Georgina Smith - Woods 10W

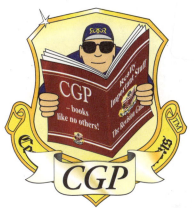

GCSE OCR 21ˢᵗ Century
Extension Science
The Revision Guide

This book is for anyone doing **GCSE OCR 21st Century Extension Science**.

GCSE Science is all about **understanding how science works**. And not only that — understanding it well enough to be able to **question** what you hear on TV and read in the papers.

But you can't do that without a fair chunk of **background knowledge**. Hmm, tricky.

Happily this CGP book includes all the **science facts** you need to learn, and shows you how they work in the **real world**. And in true CGP style, we've explained it all as **clearly and concisely** as possible.

It's also got some daft bits in to try and make the whole experience at least vaguely entertaining for you.

What CGP is all about

Our sole aim here at CGP is to produce the highest quality books — carefully written, immaculately presented and dangerously close to being funny.

Then we work our socks off to get them out to you — at the cheapest possible prices.

Contents

How Science Works

The Scientific Process 1
Risk 2

Module B7 — Further Biology

Respiration 3
Blood and Blood Typing 5
Inheritance of Blood Types 6
The Circulatory System 7
The Skeletal System 8
Health and Fitness 9
Pyramids of Numbers and Biomass 12
Energy Transfer and Energy Flow 13
Biomass in Soil 14
Symbiosis 15
Parasitism 16
Photosynthesis 17
Rate of Photosynthesis 18
Plants and Respiration 20
Humans and the Atmosphere 21
Biotechnology 22
Genetic Modification 23
DNA Technology — Genetic Testing 24
Revision Summary for Module B7 25

Module C7 — Further Chemistry

Alkanes 26
Alcohols 27
Carboxylic Acids 28
Esters 29
Making an Ester 30
Energy Transfer in Reactions 31
Catalysts and Bond Energies 32
Reversible Reactions 33
Analytical Procedures 34
Analysis — Chromatography 35
Analysis — Solution Concentrations 37

Analysis — Titration	38
The Chemical Industry	39
Producing Chemicals	40
Making Ethanol	42
Revision Summary for Module C7	44

Module P7 — Observing the Universe

Observing the Sky	45
Eclipses and the Moon	46
Coordinates in Astronomy	47
Converging Lenses	48
Telescopes	49
Astronomical Distances and Brightness	50
The Scale of the Universe	51
Gas Behaviour	53
Structure of the Atom	54
Fusion and Stellar Structure	55
Star Spectra	56
The Birth and Death of Stars	57
Observing with Telescopes	58
Space Telescopes	59
Observatories and Cooperation	60
Revision Summary for Module P7	61

Exam Skills

Extract Questions	62
Mathematical Skills	63
Drawing and Interpreting Graphs	64
Exam Skills — Paper Three	65
Index	66
Answers	68

Published by Coordination Group Publications Ltd.

Editors:
Ellen Bowness, Katherine Craig, Gemma Hallam, Sarah Hilton,
Kate Houghton, Sharon Keeley, Ali Palin, Andy Park, Katherine Reed,
David Ryan, Jane Towle, Jennifer Underwood, Julie Wakeling, Sarah Williams.

Contributors:
Michael Aicken, Mike Bossart, Mark A. Edwards, James Foster, Claire Reed,
Mike Thompson, Luke Waller, Paul Warren.

With thanks to Laura Stoney for the copyright research.

Data Source for graph of atmospheric CO_2 concentration on page 21:
C.D. Keeling and T.P. Whorf, Atmospheric CO_2 Concentrations (ppmv) derived from in situ air samples collected at Mauna Loa Observatory, Hawaii, Scripps Institute of Oceanography, August 1998.
A. Neftel et al, Historical CO_2 Record from the Siple Station Ice Core, Physics Institute, University of Bern, Switzerland, September 1994.
See http://cdiac.esd.ornl.gov/trends/co2/contents.htm

With thanks to Science Photo Library for permission to reproduce the images used on pages 55, 58, 59 and 60.

Every effort has been made to locate copyright holders and obtain permission to reproduce sources. For those sources where it has been difficult to trace the originator of the work, we would be grateful for information. If any copyright holder would like us to make an amendment to the acknowledgements, please notify us and we will gladly update the book at the next reprint. Thank you.

ISBN: 978 1 84762 329 4

Groovy website: www.cgpbooks.co.uk

Printed by Elanders Hindson Ltd, Newcastle upon Tyne.
Jolly bits of clipart from CorelDRAW®

Text, design, layout and original illustrations © Coordination Group Publications Ltd. 2009
All rights reserved.

How Science Works

The Scientific Process

This section isn't about how to 'do' science — but it does show you the way most scientists work, and how scientists try to find decent explanations for things that happen. It's pretty important stuff.

Scientists Come Up with Hypotheses...

1) Scientists try to explain things. Everything.
2) Scientists start by observing or thinking about something they don't understand. It could be anything, e.g. what matter is made of, planets in the sky, a person suffering from an illness, ... anything.
3) Then, using what they already know (plus a lot of creativity and insight), they work out an explanation (a hypothesis) that could explain what they've observed. Then they use their hypothesis to make a prediction that can be tested to provide further evidence to support the explanation. Whatever their explanation, it must stand up to the next stage of the scientific process — scrutiny from other scientists.

About 100 years ago, we thought atoms looked like this.

...Then Look for Evidence to Test Those Hypotheses

1) A hypothesis is just a theory — a belief. And believing something is true doesn't make it true — not even if you're a scientist.
2) So the next step is to try and find evidence to support the hypothesis. You might get evidence by doing controlled experiments in laboratories — a lab makes it easy to control variables so they're all kept constant (except the one you're investigating) — so it's easier to carry out a fair test.

Other Scientists Will Test the Hypotheses Too

1) Scientists report their findings to other scientists, e.g. by publishing their results in journals. Other scientists will carry out their own experiments and try to reproduce earlier results. And if all the experiments back up a hypothesis, then scientists start to have a lot of faith in it, and accept it as a theory.
2) However, if a scientist somewhere in the world gets results that don't fit with the hypothesis, either those results or the hypothesis must be wrong.
3) This process of testing a hypothesis to destruction is a vital part of the scientific process. Without the 'healthy scepticism' of scientists everywhere, we'd still believe the first theories that people came up with — like everything being made of air, water, fire or earth (or whatever).

Then we thought they looked like this.

If Evidence Supports a Hypothesis, It's Accepted — for Now

1) If pretty much every scientist in the world believes a hypothesis to be true because experiments back it up, then it usually goes in the textbooks for students to learn.
2) Our currently accepted theories are the ones that have survived this 'trial by evidence' — they've been tested many, many times over the years and survived (while the less good ones have been ditched).
3) However... they never, never become hard and fast, totally indisputable fact. You can never know... it'd only take one odd, totally inexplicable result, and the hypothesising and testing would start all over again.
4) There isn't a scientific answer to everything yet — not by a long way.

Science is a "real-world" subject...

Science isn't just about explaining things that people are curious about — if scientists can explain something that happens in the world, then maybe they can predict what will happen in the future, or even control future events — to make life a bit better in some way, either for themselves or for other people.

Risk

By reading this page you are agreeing to the risk of a paper cut or severe drowsiness that could affect your ability to operate heavy machinery... Think carefully — the choice is yours.

Nothing is Completely Risk-Free

1) Everything that you do has a risk attached to it.
2) Scientists often try to identify risks — they show correlations between certain activities (risk factors) and negative outcomes.
3) Some risks seem pretty obvious, or we've known about them for a while, like the risk of getting heart disease if you're overweight, or of having a car accident when you're travelling in a car.
4) As new technology develops it can bring new risks, e.g. some scientists believe that using a mobile phone a lot may be harmful. There are lots of risks we don't know about yet.
5) You can estimate the size of a risk based on how many times something has happened in a big sample (e.g. 100 000 people) over a given period (say, a year). The more data you have to base your assessment on, the more accurate your estimate is likely to be.
6) There are two main parts to risk — the chances of something happening and how serious the consequences would be if it did. They usually add up to give an idea of how risky an activity is. So if something is very likely to happen and there are serious consequences it's high-risk.

People Make Their Own Decisions About Risk

1) Not all risks have the same consequences, e.g. if you chop veg with a sharp knife you risk cutting your finger, but if you go scuba-diving you risk death. You're much more likely to cut your finger during half an hour of chopping than to die during half an hour of scuba-diving. But most people are happier to accept a higher probability of an accident if the consequences are short-lived and fairly minor.
2) People are also more willing to accept risks if they get a significant benefit from the activity — e.g. car travel is quite risky, but the convenience of it means that people take the risk.
3) Freedom of choice plays quite a big part, too. People tend to be more willing to accept a risk if they're choosing to do something, rather than if they're having the risk imposed on them.
4) People's perception of risk (how risky they think something is) isn't always accurate. E.g. cycling on the roads is often high-risk, but many people are still happy to do it because it's a familiar activity. Air travel is actually pretty safe, but people perceive it as high-risk, so a lot of people are afraid of it.

We Have to Choose Acceptable Levels of Risk

1) People have to choose a level of risk that they find acceptable. This varies from person to person.
2) Governments and scientists often have to choose levels of risk in various situations on behalf of other people. They'll often be influenced by public opinion though.
3) Reducing risk can cost a lot, and it's not possible to reduce any risk to zero. The people responsible aim to keep the risks As Low As Reasonably Achievable (the ALARA principle).
4) Many people react to risk using the precautionary principle (although they might not realise it...):

> **THE PRECAUTIONARY PRINCIPLE**
> If you're not sure about the risks of something, but the results could be serious and irreversible, then it makes sense to try and avoid it, e.g. we're taking action now to try and prevent/slow down climate change, even though we don't know exactly what's going to happen.

Take a risk — turn the page...

So it all boils down to the probability of something happening and the consequences if it does. You can try to reduce a risk either by making it less likely to happen or by making the consequences less severe.

How Science Works

Respiration

You need energy to live. Energy comes from the chemicals in your food — it's released by a process called respiration.

Respiration is NOT "Breathing In and Out"

1) Respiration is NOT breathing in and breathing out, as you might think.
2) Respiration actually goes on in every cell in your body.
3) It's the process of releasing energy from glucose.
4) There are two types of respiration — aerobic and anaerobic.
5) Aerobic respiration needs oxygen. Anaerobic respiration doesn't use oxygen.

This energy is used to do things like:
- build up larger molecules (like proteins)
- contract muscles
- maintain a steady body temperature

RESPIRATION is the process of RELEASING ENERGY from GLUCOSE, which happens constantly IN EVERY CELL

Aerobic Respiration Needs Plenty of Oxygen

Anaerobic respiration is covered on the next page.

1) Aerobic respiration is what happens when there's plenty of oxygen available.
2) "Aerobic" just means "with oxygen" and it releases more energy per glucose molecule than anaerobic.
3) Most of the time you're using aerobic respiration. It turns glucose from your food, and oxygen from your lungs, into carbon dioxide and water — releasing loads of energy in the process.

You need to learn the word equation:

glucose + oxygen carbon dioxide + water (+ ENERGY RELEASED)

Energy Released by Respiration is Used to Make ATP

1) ATP is a small molecule that's easily transported around cells.
2) It carries the energy released during respiration to the places where energy is needed.
3) Energy released from both aerobic and anaerobic respiration is used to produce ATP.
4) ATP is the 'energy currency' of living things.

How ATP carries energy:

1) ATP is synthesised from another molecule (called ADP) using the energy released by the breakdown of glucose during respiration.
2) ATP moves to the part of the cell that requires energy.
3) It's then broken down to ADP and this releases energy where it's needed.

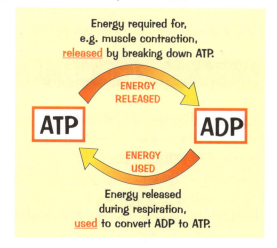

Energy required for, e.g. muscle contraction, released by breaking down ATP.

Energy released during respiration, used to convert ADP to ATP.

People say I'm greedy — I just eat out of respiration...

Isn't it strange to think that each individual living cell in your body is respiring every second of every day, releasing energy from the food you eat. Next time someone accuses you of being lazy you could claim that you're busy respiring — it's enough to make anyone feel tired.

Respiration

How <u>much</u> you respire depends on what you're doing...

You Respire More When You Exercise

1) <u>Muscles need energy</u> (<u>ATP</u>) from respiration to <u>contract</u>. When you exercise some of your muscles contract more frequently, so you need <u>more energy</u>. This energy comes from <u>increased respiration</u>.
2) The increase in respiration means you need to get <u>more oxygen</u> and glucose into the cells.
3) Your <u>breathing rate increases</u> to get more oxygen into the blood.
4) Your <u>heart rate increases</u> to get glucose and oxygenated blood around the body to your muscles quicker, and to remove CO_2 quickly at the same time.

HEART RATE

<u>Pulse rate</u> is a measure of <u>heart rate</u>. You can take someone's pulse by <u>placing two fingers</u> on their <u>wrist</u> or neck and <u>counting</u> the <u>number of pulses (heartbeats) you feel</u> in a <u>minute</u>. The normal resting heart rate range for an adult is 60-80 <u>beats/min</u>, but this will vary between individuals, e.g. the fitter you are, the lower your resting heart rate.

BLOOD PRESSURE

When heart rate increases the <u>pressure</u> of the blood also increases. The blood pressure is at its <u>highest</u> when the heart <u>contracts</u> — this is the <u>systolic pressure</u>. When the heart <u>relaxes</u>, the pressure is at its <u>lowest</u> — this is the <u>diastolic pressure</u>. Blood pressure is given as a measure of the <u>systolic pressure</u> over the <u>diastolic pressure</u>. The normal range is between <u>120/80</u> and <u>100/60</u>.

Anaerobic Respiration Doesn't Use Oxygen At All

1) When you do really <u>vigorous exercise</u> your body can't supply enough <u>oxygen</u> to your muscles for aerobic respiration — even though your <u>heart rate</u> and <u>breathing rate</u> increase as much as they can. Your muscles have to start <u>respiring anaerobically</u> as well.
2) "<u>Anaerobic</u>" just means "<u>without</u> oxygen". It's <u>NOT</u> the best way to use glucose because it releases much <u>less energy</u>. The <u>advantage</u> is that at least you can keep on using your muscles.
3) In anaerobic respiration the glucose is only <u>partially</u> broken down and <u>lactic acid</u> is also produced.

You need to learn <u>the word equation</u>:

glucose $\longrightarrow$ lactic acid (+ ENERGY RELEASED)

4) The <u>lactic acid</u> produced builds up in the muscles.
5) After resorting to anaerobic respiration, when you stop exercising you'll have an <u>oxygen debt</u>. This is the amount of <u>extra oxygen</u> you need to break down all the lactic acid that's built up in your muscles.
6) This means you have to keep <u>breathing hard</u> for a while <u>after you stop</u> exercising.
7) The lactic acid is <u>broken down</u> in your muscles and in your liver, so your <u>heart rate</u> has to <u>stay high</u> to carry the lactic acid, and the extra oxygen required to break it down, around your body.

I reckon aerobics classes should be called anaerobics instead...

OK, so when you're just sitting about, you use <u>aerobic respiration</u> to get all your energy — but when you do strenuous exercise, you can't get enough oxygen to your muscles, so you use <u>anaerobic respiration</u> too. Nothing too taxing here — just make sure you learn the equation.

Module B7 — Further Biology

Blood and Blood Typing

Blood is very useful stuff. It's a big transport system for moving things around the body, like the glucose and oxygen required for respiration. The blood cells do good work too. That's why if you lose a lot of blood it has to be replaced — that's where transfusions come in.

Blood is a Fluid Made Up of Cells, Platelets and Plasma

RED BLOOD CELLS
The job of red blood cells is to transport oxygen from the lungs to all the cells in the body.

WHITE BLOOD CELLS
They help to fight infection by protecting your body against attack from microorganisms.

PLASMA
This is the liquid that carries everything about.

PLATELETS
These are small fragments of cells that help the blood to clot at the site of a wound.

Blood Type is Important in Transfusions

1) If you're in an accident or having surgery, you may lose a lot of blood — this needs to be replaced by a blood transfusion (using blood from a blood donor). But you can't just use any old blood...
2) People have different blood types or groups — you can be any one of: A, B, O or AB. These letters refer to the type of antigens on the surface of a person's red blood cells. (An antigen is a substance that can trigger a response from a person's immune system.)
3) Red blood cells can have A or B antigens (or neither, or both) on their surface.
4) And blood plasma can contain anti-A or anti-B antibodies (antibodies are proteins produced by the immune system).
5) If anti-A antibodies meet A antigens OR anti-B antibodies meet B antigens the blood will clot.
6) So before people are given a blood transfusion they are tested to check what type they are.
7) This table should make everything lovely and clear...

Blood Type	Antigens	Antibodies	Can give blood to	Can get blood from
A	A	anti-B	A and AB	A and O
B	B	anti-A	B and AB	B and O
AB	A, B	none	only AB	anyone
O	none	anti-A, anti-B	anyone	only O

For example, 'O blood' can be given to anyone — there are no antigens on the blood cells, so any anti-A or anti-B antibodies have nothing to 'attack'.

I think I need an information transfusion... from this book to my brain...

You might get asked a question on who can donate blood to whom (or vice versa) in the exam. Just look at what blood type the donor is and think about what antigens and antibodies they have in their blood. It's hard, and you need to think carefully about it (I do anyway) but it does make sense.

Inheritance of Blood Types

Your blood type depends on the genes you've inherited from your parents.
Inheritance of blood types is a bit more complicated than examples you've looked at before...

The Gene for Blood Type has Three Alleles

1) Alleles are different versions of the same gene.
2) Most inheritance you will have studied involved two alleles (versions) of one gene, but there are more than two alleles of some genes.
3) ABO blood type is determined by a single gene that has three alleles:

I^O is the allele for blood type O. I^A is the allele for blood type A. I^B is the allele for blood type B.

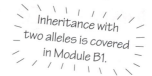

Inheritance with two alleles is covered in Module B1.

Alleles Can be Co-dominant

1) Usually, when you have two different alleles the characteristic that shows (phenotype) is caused by the dominant allele and the other allele is said to be recessive. But it doesn't always happen like this...
2) Some alleles are co-dominant — the phenotype is a mix of the characteristics from both alleles.
3) With ABO blood types the alleles I^A and I^B are co-dominant and I^O is recessive to both I^A and I^B. So, if you have the genotype $I^A I^B$ your phenotype will be blood type AB — e.g. you'll have both A and B antigens on the surface of your red blood cells.
4) This means there are four possible blood types:

Your genotype is what alleles you have, e.g. $I^O I^O$.
Your phenotype is the characteristics you have, e.g. blood type O.

Blood Type	Alleles
A	$I^A I^A$ OR $I^A I^O$
B	$I^B I^B$ OR $I^B I^O$
AB	$I^A I^B$
O	$I^O I^O$

Remember, I^O is recessive so you need two I^O alleles to be blood type O.

This blood type shows characteristics of both alleles.

You Need to be Able to Draw and Interpret Genetic Diagrams

If a couple know their own blood type genotypes they can work out the possible blood types of their kids using a genetic diagram. For example, if one person is blood type A genotype $I^A I^O$, and the other is blood type B genotype $I^B I^O$, their kids could have one of four different blood types:

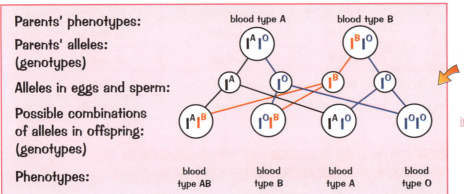

You draw the diagram in the same way as you do for inheritance with only two alleles — it's only how you interpret the characteristics from the alleles at the end that's different.

My sister's BO — she does whiff a bit...

They might ask you to draw or interpret a genetic diagram in the exam — so make sure you understand how they work and which combinations of alleles result in each of the four blood types, A, B, AB and O.

Module B7 — Further Biology

The Circulatory System

The circulatory system is everything to do with your heart and your blood. It's the circulatory system that takes digested food and oxygen around the body and removes the waste products from your tissues.

Humans Have a Double Circulatory System

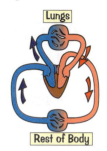

1) Humans have a double circulatory system — two circuits joined together.
2) The first one pumps deoxygenated blood (blood without oxygen) to the lungs to take in oxygen. The blood then returns to the heart.
3) The second one pumps oxygenated blood around the body. The blood gives up its oxygen at the body cells and the deoxygenated blood returns to the heart to be pumped out to the lungs again.

Learn This Diagram of the Heart with All Its Labels

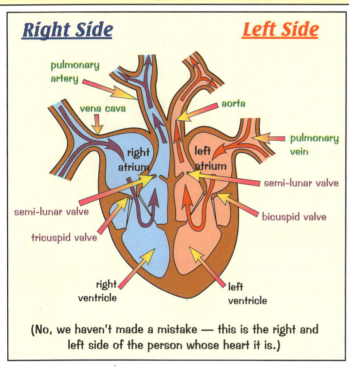

(No, we haven't made a mistake — this is the right and left side of the person whose heart it is.)

1) The right atrium of the heart receives deoxygenated blood from the body (through the vena cava).
2) The deoxygenated blood moves through to the right ventricle, which pumps it to the lungs (via the pulmonary artery).
3) The left atrium receives oxygenated blood from the lungs (through the pulmonary vein).
4) The oxygenated blood then moves through to the left ventricle, which pumps it out round the whole body (via the aorta).
5) The left ventricle has a much thicker wall than the right ventricle. It needs more muscle because it has to pump blood around the whole body, whereas the right ventricle only has to pump it to the lungs.
6) The semi-lunar, tricuspid and bicuspid valves prevent the backflow of blood. Veins also have valves to prevent the backflow of blood.

Chemicals are Exchanged Between Cells and Capillaries

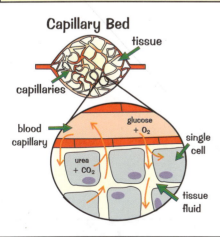

1) Arteries branch into capillaries, which are really tiny blood vessels.
2) They have permeable walls, so substances can diffuse in and out.
3) Networks of capillaries in tissue are called capillary beds.
4) As blood passes through capillary beds small molecules (e.g. water, glucose and oxygen) are forced out of the capillaries to form the tissue fluid, which surrounds the cells. These substances can then diffuse out of the tissue fluid into the cells.
5) Waste chemicals (e.g. carbon dioxide and urea) diffuse out of the cells into the tissue fluid, then into the capillaries.
6) The tissue fluid allows cells to get the substances they need and get rid of waste without a capillary supplying every single cell.

The heart — it's all just pump and circumstance...

There's more on the brilliant circulatory system in Module B2. You need to know it all, so get learnin'.

Module B7 — Further Biology

The Skeletal System

Your blood carries the glucose your body needs to release energy for things like movement. But you do need other things to move — bones and joints are pretty darned important too.

If You Didn't Have a Skeleton, You'd be Jelly-like

1) The job of a skeleton is to support the body and allow it to move — as well as protect vital organs.
2) Fish, amphibians, reptiles, birds and mammals are all vertebrates — they all have a backbone and an internal skeleton. Other animals (e.g. insects) have their skeleton on the outside.

Joints Allow the Bones to Move

1) The bones at a joint are held together by ligaments. Ligaments have tensile strength (i.e. you can pull them and they don't snap easily) but they are also slightly elastic (stretchy).
2) The ends of bones are covered with a smooth layer of cartilage to stop the bones rubbing together. Cartilage can be slightly compressed so it acts as a shock absorber, like a cushion between bones.
3) Membranes at some joints release oily synovial fluid to lubricate the joints, allowing them to move more easily.
4) Different kinds of joints move in different ways.

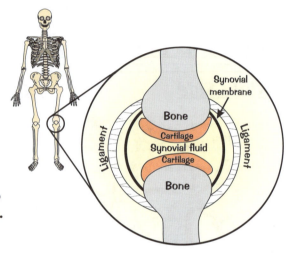

Muscles Pull on Bones to Move Them

1) Bones are attached to muscles by tendons (which also attach muscles to other muscles).
2) Muscles move bones at a joint by contracting (becoming shorter).
3) Tendons can't stretch much so when a muscle contracts it pulls on the bone.
4) Muscles can only pull on bones to move a joint — they can't push. This is why muscles usually come in pairs (called antagonistic pairs).
5) When one muscle in the pair contracts, the joint moves in one direction. When the other muscle contracts, it moves in the opposite direction. Here's an example:

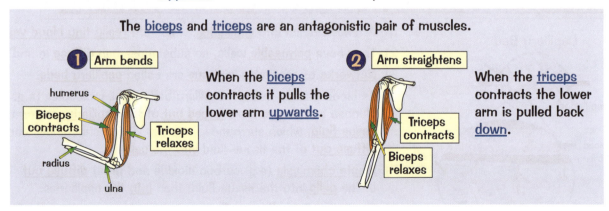

What's a skeleton's favourite instrument?... a trom-bone...

Different joints have different ranges of movement. And if you do something that makes the bone move further than its normal range of movement (like fall on it), then you could dislocate it. Painful.

Module B7 — Further Biology

Health and Fitness

These next three pages cover a bit about the work of health and fitness practitioners. Health practitioners, e.g. doctors, nurses and physiotherapists, deal with the treatment of illness and injury. Fitness practitioners, e.g. personal trainers and gym instructors, deal with healthy people who want to improve their fitness.

Patients Need Regular Contact with Practitioners

It's important for health and fitness practitioners to monitor their patients for a variety of reasons:

Health practitioners
1) To check medication is working and if necessary re-evaluate the treatment — e.g. they can retest the patient to see if they still have an infection.
2) To check for side effects from the treatment.

Fitness practitioners
1) To provide encouragement — this helps to keep the client motivated.
2) To monitor progress and adjust the aims if necessary — e.g. increase the distance run in a set time.
3) To check for injuries — in case the client is overdoing it.

Information is Needed to Develop the Right Treatment Regimes

Practitioners need to have essential background information, such as:

1) Symptoms — if the patient needs medical treatment the practitioner needs to know what symptoms they have, to diagnose them and to help choose a suitable treatment.
2) Previous health or fitness treatments — to know what has or hasn't worked before.
3) Family medical history — illnesses often run in families, so it could be important for diagnosis.

4) Other lifestyle factors — e.g. a patient who smokes or drinks heavily may be more likely to suffer from certain diseases or disorders.
5) Current medication — different medicines can sometimes interact so it's important to know what patients are already taking to avoid this.
6) Physical activity — this usually only applies when planning a fitness programme. It allows the practitioners to plan a challenging programme that won't injure the client.

Practitioners Need to Keep Records

Practitioners always keep records of their clients' details. This is important for:

- remembering the essential background information they used to plan the programme or treatment — they'll see lots of clients and it'd be hard to remember everyone's details.
- remembering the treatment or fitness plan.
- monitoring changes — to see if the client is making progress.
- sharing information — most professionals work as part of a larger team, e.g. doctors may work with physiotherapists and nurses. It's important that all the members of the team can look at all the information so they know what treatment or programme has been advised and can assist in the care of the patient or client.

My idea of a fitness programme — running to the pie shop...

It can be really important to see your health or fitness practitioner often when you're trying to stick to a personal programme. Sometimes repeated exercises can get boring (just like revising) and a bit of encouragement can make a big difference. Now go work those brain cells and learn this page.

Module B7 — Further Biology

Health and Fitness

There are lots of things to think about when choosing a treatment or designing a fitness programme.

Treatments Can Have Side Effects

Treatments are designed to increase the rate of healing and to reduce the chances of further damage. But some treatments can also have damaging side effects. The benefits and side effects are weighed against each other, and as long as the benefits outweigh the side effects then the treatment will continue.

There is Usually More Than One Way to Achieve a Target

Different treatments and fitness programmes may have different targets, for example:
1) Enhanced fitness — when the client is aiming to improve their fitness. This might mean different things for different people, e.g. running faster or increasing flexibility.
2) Cure — often the repair of damaged tissues, e.g. the healing of a sprained ligament or mending a broken bone. Often, a cure can be brought about by natural healing, if the affected part is rested.
3) Recovery and Rehabilitation — when the patient is brought back to the same level of function and fitness as before an injury or illness. This might involve a training programme where the patient undertakes progressively more difficult tasks, slowly rebuilding their strength or flexibility.

Treatments or programmes are tailored for each patient or client. Different methods are often used to reach the same target in separate patients, for example:

> A young man has broken his hip. A doctor has advised pain relief and rest to let the bone mend, followed by physiotherapy, to increase his muscle strength around the hip and to increase his mobility. An elderly man has also broken his hip. A doctor has advised a hip replacement, followed by rest to recover from the surgery and physiotherapy to build up muscle strength and mobility around the joint.

The Treatment May Need to be Modified

During the monitoring process a practitioner may notice something that means the treatment or fitness programme needs to be modified. Here are some of the reasons why it might be modified:
1) Because it's not producing any improvement, e.g. an antibiotic isn't clearing an infection.
2) Because it's causing damage, e.g. exercises that are too difficult and are causing injury.
3) Because it's producing side effects that are dangerous or outweigh the benefits, e.g. patients with arthritis are often prescribed aspirin but this can sometimes lead to bad stomach problems.

After a treatment is completed, monitoring should still continue — to check improvement is maintained.

> For example, an athlete has torn her heel tendon. She has to rest it and then start a series of exercises, gradually stretching the heel more and more. Her trainer regularly checks and records the amount of stretch at the heel and checks for signs that the tear is getting worse — like stiffness or pain. The athlete will be monitored for a few weeks after the treatment is complete to make sure everything is still OK.

Assessment of progress always depends on the accuracy and reliability of the monitoring procedures —

ACCURACY — the results should be as close to what's actually happening as possible, e.g. if a doctor is monitoring someone's weight they need to be sure the scales they are using are accurate.

RELIABILITY — the results should be consistent, e.g. again when monitoring someone's weight, they should be weighed on the same scales and wearing the same amount of clothes to get a fair comparison.

Boredom — the dangerous side effect of revision...

Sorry, not a lot of fun stuff on this page — but you've still got to learn it, learn it, learn it.

Module B7 — Further Biology

Health and Fitness

Although exercise is great for your health and fitness, too much of it can cause problems...

Excessive Exercising Can Cause Injuries

Some common injuries that can result from excessive exercise are:

1) Sprains — damage to a ligament (see page 8), usually by being stretched too much. E.g. a "twisted ankle" is where the foot turns over, pulling the ligament too far, causing damage and pain.

2) Dislocations — a bone comes out of its socket (eek). For example, a heavy fall could cause a dislocation at the shoulder, causing severe pain. It also makes the joint look weird (because the bone is in the wrong position).

3) Torn ligaments — the ligament actually tears. This will cause more severe pain than a sprain and will often mean loss of control of the joint because the bones are no longer attached firmly together.

4) Torn tendons — a tear in the tendon that attaches the muscle to its bone. It occurs when a muscle contracts in one direction, but is being pulled in the opposite direction. And it's painful too.

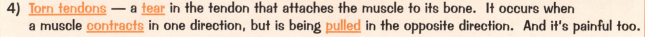

The RICE Method Can be Used to Treat Sprains

The main symptoms of a sprain are pain and swelling in the affected area. Treatment involves reducing these symptoms and creating the right conditions for the injury to heal itself. If a sprain is not too severe, it can be treated using the RICE method:

Rest — to avoid any further damage. This is especially important for the first 24 hours. Then, the joint can be slowly and progressively used more and more.

Ice — to help to reduce swelling (e.g. using a bag of frozen peas wrapped in a tea towel!). It works by reducing the temperature and blood flow to the injured area.

Compression — a firm bandage is placed around the injured part to help reduce swelling and prevent further damage from excessive movement of the injured joint. You have to make sure it's not too tight or it'll cut off the blood flow to the area.

Elevation — raising an injured limb as high as possible to help reduce swelling by making it easier for blood to flow back to the heart.

Physiotherapists Treat Skeletal-muscular Injuries

More serious injuries to the skeletal or muscular system will be treated by a physiotherapist. A physiotherapist may give treatment to reduce pain and swelling (e.g. RICE, cortisone injections) and therapies (e.g. laser treatment) to speed up healing. They will also advise on the best exercises to do to rehabilitate after an injury. These may be graded exercises, which steadily build up the strength of a muscle or joint. For example, for a damaged knee, the exercise might consist of —

1) Standing up and tensing the muscles without moving the knee.
2) Sitting with the lower leg hanging loose, then slowly raising and lowering the lower leg by bending the knee.
3) Stepping up and down, onto and off a low box.
4) Standing, and bending and straightening the legs at the knees.

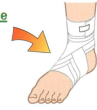

Not guilty — the sporting verdict in juries...

Make sure you can recall every injury given here and know the symptoms and how to treat a sprain.

Module B7 — Further Biology

Pyramids of Numbers and Biomass

And now for something completely different... plants and animals... lovely. Food chains show the feeding relationships between different species — which organisms are eating what, basically. You can illustrate a food chain by drawing a pyramid of numbers or a pyramid of biomass.

Pyramids of Numbers are a Way of Showing Food Chains

Here's an example of a food chain:

5000 dandelions... feed... 100 rabbits... which feed... 1 fox.

1) Each stage of a food chain is called a trophic (feeding) level — in this one the rabbits are the second trophic level. Each bar on a pyramid of numbers shows the total number of organisms at that level of the food chain.
2) So the 'dandelions' bar on this pyramid would need to be longer than the 'rabbits' bar, which in turn should be longer than the 'fox' bar.
3) Dandelions go at the bottom because they're at the bottom of the food chain. Dandelions, like all plants, are producers — they convert light into energy which they can use to grow (see page 17).
4) In a typical pyramid of numbers every time you go up a trophic level, the number of organisms goes down. This is because a big organism will usually need to eat lots of smaller organisms to stay alive.

Pyramids of numbers have the advantage of being simple to produce — you just count the number of organisms at each level. They can be misleading though — the nice pyramid shape is often messed up by the presence of small numbers of big organisms (like trees) or large numbers of small organisms (like fleas).

Pyramids of Biomass Give a More Accurate Picture

1) Each bar on a pyramid of biomass shows the mass of living material at that stage of the food chain — basically how much all the organisms at each level would weigh if you put them all together. So one tree would have a big biomass and hundreds of fleas would have a small biomass.
2) The advantage of pyramids of biomass is that they give a fairly accurate indication of the amount of energy at each level in the food chain. They are nearly always a proper pyramid:

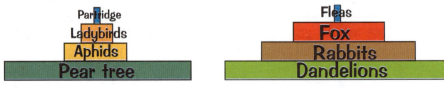

3) Pyramids of biomass don't show you the number of organisms in each layer — but you can use your common sense to make a rough guess. E.g. in the diagram on the left, lots (probably thousands) of aphids are feeding on a small number of trees.

Constructing pyramids is a breeze — just ask the Egyptians...

There are actually a couple of exceptions where pyramids of biomass aren't quite pyramid-shaped. It happens when the producer has a very short life but reproduces loads, like with plankton at certain times of year. But it's rare, and you don't need to know about it. Forget I ever mentioned it. Sorry.

Module B7 — Further Biology

Energy Transfer and Energy Flow

Energy is Transferred Between Organisms in an Ecosystem

1) Energy from the <u>Sun</u> is the source of energy for nearly <u>all</u> life on Earth.

2) <u>Plants</u> use a small percentage of the light energy from the Sun to make <u>food</u> during photosynthesis. This energy is stored in the chemicals which make up the plants' cells (see page 17). Organisms that are able to <u>produce</u> their own food in this way are called <u>autotrophs</u>.

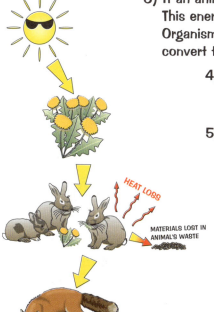

3) If an animal eats a plant, then it <u>takes in the energy</u> stored in the plant. This energy then works its way through the <u>food web</u> as animals eat each other. Organisms that <u>gain</u> their energy in this way are called <u>heterotrophs</u>. They can't convert the Sun's energy into food — they're <u>reliant on autotrophs</u> to do this.

4) <u>Decomposers</u> (e.g. some bacteria and fungi) feed on <u>dead animals and plants</u> and animal <u>droppings</u>. This is another way in which energy is transferred between organisms.

5) <u>Energy passes out</u> of the food chain <u>at each trophic level</u>. This is because:
   - Some energy is used in <u>respiration</u> (see page 3), which powers all life processes.
   - Some energy is <u>lost</u> to the surroundings as <u>heat</u>.
   - Some energy is lost in <u>animal droppings</u>.

   The <u>energy</u> that <u>passes out</u> of the food chain isn't made into <u>biomass</u>, so this energy isn't available to the <u>next trophic level</u>.

   <u>Energy</u> also <u>passes out</u> of the food chain <u>between</u> each trophic level. This is because:
   - Some <u>material isn't eaten</u> (e.g. bones), so the energy stored in it <u>isn't passed</u> on to the next trophic level.

6) This is why you rarely get <u>food chains</u> with more than <u>five trophic levels</u>. So much <u>energy</u> is <u>lost</u> at (and between) each stage that there's not enough left to support more organisms after four or five stages.

You Need to be Able to Calculate the Efficiency of Energy Transfer

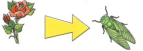

rosebush: 80 000 kJ   greenfly: 10 000 kJ   ladybird: 900 kJ   bird: 40 kJ

A kilojoule (kJ) is just a measure of energy.

1) The numbers show the <u>amount of energy</u> available to the <u>next level</u>. So <u>80 000 kJ</u> is the amount of energy available to the <u>greenfly</u>, and <u>10 000 kJ</u> is the amount available to the <u>ladybird</u>.

2) At each level, <u>energy is lost</u> and the <u>amount available</u> for the <u>next level</u> in the food chain <u>decreases</u>.

3) You can calculate the <u>percentage efficiency of energy transfer</u> at each stage of the food chain — this means how good the food chain is at passing energy from one level to the next.

$$\% \text{ efficiency} = \frac{\text{energy available to the next level}}{\text{energy that was available to the previous level}} \times 100$$

So between the 1st and 2nd trophic level, <u>efficiency</u> of energy transfer = 10 000 kJ ÷ 80 000 kJ × 100
= <u>12.5% efficient</u>.

To lose 1 kJ of energy is a misfortune, to lose 2 kJ is careless...

Some energy is used up at every trophic level — this energy isn't used to make new biomass. This explains why you get biomass pyramids (see last page) — there's less biomass at each stage.

Module B7 — Further Biology

Biomass in Soil

Soil contains biomass in the form of wriggly, horrible creatures and bugs. These creatures are pretty important in food chains as they break down material into nutrients that plants (the producers for pretty much all food chains) can use.

Soil Contains Four Main Things

Soil isn't just mud. It contains four main components, and different amounts of these can affect how good the soil is for growing plants.

1) Inorganic material — this includes broken up pieces of rock (mineral particles) and mineral ions dissolved in the water in the soil.
2) Biomass — living and dead organic matter. Many organisms live in the soil (e.g. earthworms, insects and bacteria). You also find dead organic matter in the soil — called humus. This consists of dead earthworms, insects etc. and fallen leaves and other dead vegetation.
3) Water — this is retained on the surfaces of the mineral particles. It's vital for growing plants.
4) Air — this is contained in tiny spaces between the mineral particles. The oxygen in the air is vital for the respiration of soil animals and plant roots.

You Need to be Able to Calculate the Amount of Water in Soil...

Because water is so important for plant growth, people (like farmers) may want to find out how much water there is in their soil. Here's how you do it...

1) Weigh a dish.
2) Put a sample of soil in the dish and weigh the whole thing (dish + soil).
3) Heat the dish and soil in an oven at a temperature between 90 °C and 110 °C — hot enough to evaporate off all the water without burning off any of the organic matter.
4) Let it cool and weigh it again.
5) Repeat the heating and weighing until the weight doesn't go down any more (so you know you've really got rid of all the water).
6) Calculate the percentage mass of water in the soil like this.

> Mass of dish = 30 g
> Mass of dish + soil before heating = 150 g
> So, the mass of the soil before heating must be
>   = 150 − 30 = 120 g
> Mass of dish + soil after heating = 130 g
> So, the mass of the soil after heating must be
>   = 130 − 30 = 100 g
> The mass of water in the soil is the same as the weight lost during heating = 120 g − 100 g = 20 g
> So, percentage of water in the soil
>   = (20 ÷ 120) × 100 = 16.7%

...and the Amount of Biomass

Once you've worked out the percentage of water in the soil, you can have even more fun, calculating the amount of biomass. This is what to do...

1) First carry out the method above to remove all the water in the soil.
2) Heat the soil sample strongly in a crucible over a Bunsen burner to burn off all the biomass.
3) Cool it, weigh it, and heat again until the mass stays constant. Record the final weight.
4) Calculate the percentage of biomass like this.

> Mass of soil after heating to remove water = 100 g
> Mass of soil after burning off biomass = 70 g
> The mass of organic matter is equal to the weight lost during strong heating = 100 g − 70 g = 30 g
> So, percentage of organic matter in the soil
>   = (30 ÷ 100) × 100 = 30%

Soil contains all-sorts — Roman remains, buried treasure...

Make sure you remember the four main things that soil contains — there are some easy marks to be had. It's really important that you know how to calculate the amount of water and biomass in a soil sample. Work your way through the examples on this page so you understand what's being done at each stage.

Module B7 — Further Biology

Symbiosis

This page is all about 'nutritional interactions' between species. Sounds exciting? That's because it is.

Symbiosis — Living Together in Direct Contact

In the natural environment, some organisms of different species live together in close contact with each other — this is called symbiosis (they have a symbiotic relationship). There are different kinds of symbiotic relationships, which have different impacts on the organisms involved:

1) Commensalism — this is a relationship where one organism benefits but the other (the host) is neither helped nor harmed.
2) Parasitism — in this close association one organism benefits (the parasite) and the other is harmed (the host).

You need to be able to recognise examples of commensalism for your exam. And you also need to know lots more about parasites...

E.g. the relationship between a hermit crab and an organism commonly found attached to its shell, called a hydroid. The hydroid obtains food particles from the crab — the hydroid benefits but the crab neither benefits nor loses.

Other examples include when an organism uses the host as a form of transport or as housing.

Parasites Have Special Features That Help Them Survive

Parasites have evolved specific features that enable them to be successful in their host. The tapeworm and blood fluke are great examples of how parasites are adapted...

Tapeworms

Some tapeworms can cause disease in humans. They're adapted to absorb the digested food in the intestines of humans. They have...

1) A large surface area, so digested food can move into their body by diffusion.
2) Hooks or suckers which help them to attach and hold on to the walls of the intestines.

The tapeworm has no intestines — it simply doesn't need any. It just lies about and absorbs digested food.

Blood flukes

Blood flukes can cause liver damage. Some have evolved the following adaptations to infect humans...

1) A pointed head — this allows them to burrow through the skin and enter the host.
2) They can incorporate human antigens (Module B2) onto their surface — making them 'invisible' to the host's immune system.

Blood flukes live in lakes — they can infect people standing or swimming in the water.

Don't worry — they're not lurking in lakes in the UK.

Parasites can affect us in several ways...

1) Some parasites can cause disease in humans, e.g. malaria (see next page). Parasitic diseases cause a huge amount of pain and suffering and cost a lot of money to treat.
2) Parasites can seriously affect food production. They can damage crops and cause disease in livestock — decreasing yield. Parasite damage is thought to have a huge economic impact world wide.

The evolution of a parasite is thought to be closely linked to that of its host. This makes sense when you think about it — as the host evolves ways to prevent infection or destroy the parasite, the parasite in turn will evolve ways to avoid the host's mechanisms.

Fish & chips — a perfect symbiotic relationship

The evolution of a parasite and its host is a bit like a race to make the better weapon. For example, a caveman might've invented a big club, so the other caveman (yep, there were only two) invented the spear, and maybe a helmet so that the club didn't hurt quite so much. It'll probably go on forever.

Module B7 — Further Biology

Parasitism

As you saw on the previous page, parasites can cause some horrid human diseases. Some of these diseases can even have an effect on the genetic make-up of populations...

Malaria is a Human Disease Caused by a Parasite

The parasitic microorganism that causes malaria is spread by mosquitoes.
It's one of the most widespread infectious diseases in the world — it has a huge impact in Africa.
A lot of people in the African population also suffer from the genetic disease sickle-cell anaemia.
Is this simply a coincidence or is there an extremely interesting explanation? I bet you'd love to know...

Sickle-Cell Anaemia Affects Red Blood Cells

1) Sickle-cell anaemia is a genetic disorder that causes the red blood cells to be shaped like sickles instead of the normal round shape.
2) These red blood cells can get stuck in the capillaries, which deprives body cells of oxygen.
3) It's an unpleasant, painful disorder and sufferers are at risk of dying at an early age.
4) Symptoms include physical weakness, pain, fever, anaemia and even heart failure and brain damage.
5) Sickle-cell anaemia can be treated with a bone marrow transplant (see your Module B1 notes) and some of the symptoms can be prevented by drugs and blood transfusions.

Sickle-Cell Anaemia is Caused by a Faulty Recessive Allele

Sickle-cell anaemia is caused by inheriting two recessive alleles 'a' (for anaemia). The normal allele is represented by an 'A'.

If two people who carry the sickle cell anaemia allele have children, the probability of each child suffering from the disorder is 1 in 4 — 25%. The most likely ratio in the children is 3:1, non-sufferer:sufferer.

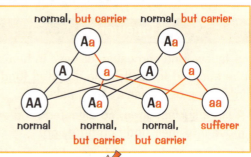

A carrier of sickle-cell anaemia is a person who has only one recessive allele.
Carriers are normally healthy but can pass on the sickle-cell allele to their children.

Carriers Have Some Protection from Malaria

1) Sickle-cell anaemia is rare in Britain, but not in some African countries. This is because carriers are more immune to malaria.
2) The malaria parasites use red blood cells as a place to grow and divide. Some of the red blood cells of carriers are abnormal. The parasites find it difficult to live in these abnormal red blood cells — so carriers are less likely to get malaria.
3) So, a carrier has an increased chance of survival in the parts of the world where malaria is common, even though some of their offspring may suffer from sickle-cell anaemia. Carriers are more likely to survive and reproduce to pass on their genes — including the sickle-cell allele.
4) Natural selection has caused the sickle cell allele to be more frequent in these populations because of this survival advantage. (There's more on natural selection in Module B3.)

The sickle-cell allele is caused by a small mutation (change) in DNA.

Disease can influence the evolution of a population...

Sickle-cell anaemia is a great example of natural selection in action. Normally, recessive genetic diseases are pretty rare in a population. People who have the disease might not survive to produce offspring — they won't pass on their genetic material, making the allele less frequent in the population.

Module B7 — Further Biology

Photosynthesis

Plants can make their own food — it's ace. Here's how...

Plants Produce Glucose by Photosynthesis

1) Photosynthesis is the process that produces 'food' in plants. The 'food' it produces is glucose — a sugar.
2) Photosynthesis happens in the leaves of all green plants — this is largely what the leaves are for.
3) Photosynthesis happens inside the chloroplasts, which are found in leaf cells and in other green parts of a plant. Chloroplasts contain a substance called chlorophyll, which absorbs sunlight and allows its energy to be used to convert carbon dioxide and water into glucose. Oxygen is also produced.

Learn the equation for photosynthesis:

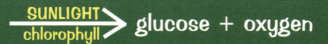

$$\text{carbon dioxide} + \text{water} \xrightarrow[\text{chlorophyll}]{\text{SUNLIGHT}} \text{glucose} + \text{oxygen}$$

Plants Use the Glucose in Three Main Ways

① Glucose is Used for Respiration

1) Plants use some of the glucose for respiration (see page 3).
2) This process releases energy from the glucose. Some of this energy is used to convert some of the glucose into various other useful substances which they can use to build new cells and grow.
3) To produce some of these substances they also need to gather minerals from the soil.

② Glucose is Used to Make Chemicals for Growth

1) Glucose is converted into cellulose for making cell walls, especially in a rapidly growing plant.
2) Glucose is combined with nitrates (collected from the soil) to make amino acids, which are then made into proteins.
3) Glucose is also used to help make chlorophyll.

③ Glucose is Stored as Starch

1) Glucose is turned into starch and stored in roots, stems and leaves, ready for use at times when the rate of photosynthesis is slower, like in the winter. Potato and carrot plants store a lot of starch underground over the winter so a new plant can grow from it the following spring.
2) Starch is insoluble in water, which makes it much better for storing because it doesn't bloat the storage cells by osmosis like glucose would (glucose is soluble in water).

So, plants can use glucose to make cellulose, proteins and starch, which are all polymers.

Convert this page into stored information...

Without plants we'd all be pretty stuffed really — plants are able to use the Sun's energy glucose. This is the energy source which humans and all other animals need for respiration Make sure you know the photosynthesis equation inside out — it's important later in the sec

Module B7 — Furthe

Rate of Photosynthesis

The rate of photosynthesis is affected by environmental conditions...

Three Factors Affect the Rate of Photosynthesis

1) There are three factors that can affect the rate of photosynthesis...

   1) amount of light
   2) amount of CO_2
   3) temperature

2) Any of these three factors can become the limiting factor. This just means that it stops photosynthesis from happening any faster.

Plants also need water but if water is so low that it becomes the limiting factor, the plant's probably already nearly dead.

3) Which factor is limiting at a particular time depends on the environmental conditions:
   - at night it's pretty obvious that light is the limiting factor,
   - in winter it's often the temperature,
   - if it's warm enough and bright enough, the amount of CO_2 is usually limiting.

Three Important Graphs for Rate of Photosynthesis

1) Not Enough Light Slows Down the Rate of Photosynthesis

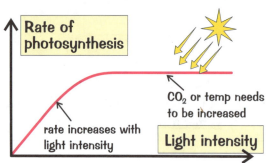

1) Light provides the energy needed for photosynthesis.
2) As the light level is raised, the rate of photosynthesis increases steadily — but only up to a certain point.
3) Beyond that, it won't make any difference because then it'll be either the temperature or the CO_2 level which is the limiting factor.
4) When investigating the rate of photosynthesis (see next page) you can change the light intensity by moving a lamp closer to or further away from your plant.

5) But if you just plot the rate of photosynthesis against "distance of lamp from the plant" in an experiment, you get a weird-shaped graph. To get a graph like the one above you either need to measure the light intensity at the beaker using a light meter or do a bit of nifty maths with your results.

2) Too Little Carbon Dioxide Also Slows It Down

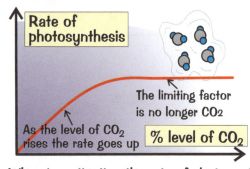

1) CO_2 is one of the raw materials needed for photosynthesis.
2) As with light intensity, the amount of CO_2 will only increase the rate of photosynthesis up to a point. After this the graph flattens out, showing that CO_2 is no longer the limiting factor.
3) As long as light and CO_2 are in plentiful supply then the factor limiting photosynthesis must be temperature.

4) When investigating the rate of photosynthesis (see next page) there are loads of different ways to control the amount of CO_2. If you're using water plants in your experiment you could dissolve different amounts of sodium hydrogencarbonate in the water, which gives off CO_2.

Don't blame it on the sunshine, don't blame it on the CO_2...

...don't blame it on the temperature, blame it on the plant. Right, now you'll never forget the three limiting factors in photosynthesis. No... well, make sure you read these two pages over and over again till you do. With your newly found knowledge of photosynthesis you could take over the world...

Rate of Photosynthesis

3) The Temperature Has to be Just Right

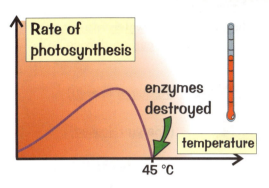

1) Usually, if the temperature is the limiting factor it's because it's too low — the enzymes needed for photosynthesis work more slowly at low temperatures.
2) But if the plant gets too hot, the enzymes it needs for photosynthesis and its other reactions will be denatured (see your Module B4 notes).
3) This happens at about 45 °C (which is pretty hot for outdoors, although greenhouses can get that hot if you're not careful).

So the amount of light, carbon dioxide and the temperature can all affect the rate of photosynthesis. There's a pretty easy way to test this...

You can Measure the Rate Under Different Conditions

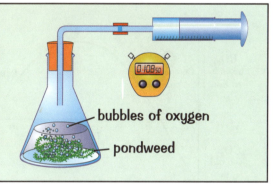

You can do experiments to work out the ideal conditions for photosynthesis in a particular plant. The easiest type to use is a water plant like Canadian pondweed — you can easily measure the amount of oxygen produced in a given time to show how fast photosynthesis is happening (remember — oxygen is made during photosynthesis).

You could either count the bubbles given off, or if you want to be a bit more accurate, you could collect the oxygen in a gas syringe.

Only Change One Variable at a Time

When you're doing an experiment, you have to try and keep all the variables (factors) constant apart from the one you're investigating, so it's a fair test. E.g. if you're testing how light affects the rate of photosynthesis you should make sure the plant has enough CO_2 and it's at a decent temperature. If your experiment's not a fair test then your results won't be reliable.

There's a couple of things you should look out for...

1) If you want to change the intensity of the light, make sure your light source doesn't increase the temperature (lamps give out heat as well as light).
2) If you put your plant in the dark make sure the temperature isn't different — a dark cupboard could be colder than the rest of the room.
3) Make sure you use a large flask, and do the experiments as quickly as you can, so that the plant doesn't use up too much of the CO_2 in the flask. If you're using sodium hydrogencarbonate as your CO_2 source, make sure it's changed each time.

Number of cups of tea — that's my limiting factor...

You can create the best conditions for photosynthesis in a greenhouse. Farmers use heaters and artificial lights and they can also increase the level of CO_2 using paraffin burners. By keeping plants in a greenhouse, they're also keeping out pests and diseases. The plants will grow much more quickly.

Module B7 — Further Biology

Plants and Respiration

Plant cells respire to release energy — just like animal cells (see page 3).

Respiration Releases the Energy in Glucose

1) Plants use photosynthesis to trap light energy and turn carbon dioxide and water into oxygen and glucose. Respiration uses oxygen and glucose and turns it back into carbon dioxide and water. These are opposite processes...

> Photosynthesis: carbon dioxide + water → glucose + oxygen   (Requires energy)

> Respiration: glucose + oxygen → carbon dioxide + water   (Energy released)

2) Photosynthesis only happens during the day. But plants respire all the time, day and night.
3) During the day, plants make more oxygen by photosynthesis than they use in respiration. So in daylight, they take in carbon dioxide from the surrounding atmosphere and release oxygen.
4) At night though, plants only respire — there's no light for photosynthesis. This means they take in oxygen from the surrounding atmosphere and release carbon dioxide.
5) The graph below shows how the amount of carbon dioxide taken in or released by a plant varies over a 24-hour period...

The graph for oxygen will be the exact opposite of the graph for CO_2 below.

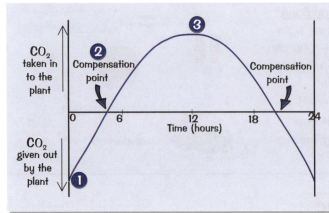

① At midnight the rate of photosynthesis is zero (as it is dark) — more carbon dioxide is being given out by respiration than is used up.

② Compensation point — the amount of CO_2 released by respiration is equal to the amount the plant uses for photosynthesis.

③ The rate of photosynthesis is highest at midday — the plant is taking in a lot more carbon dioxide for photosynthesis than it's giving out from respiration.

Energy from Respiration is Used for Active Transport

1) Some of the cells on plant roots grow into long 'hairs' which stick out into the soil.
2) Root hairs give the plant a big surface area for absorbing minerals from the soil. Minerals are essential for growth.
3) But the concentration of minerals in the soil is usually pretty low. It's normally higher in the root hair cell than in the soil around it.
4) So normal diffusion doesn't explain how minerals are taken up into the root hair cell. They should go the other way if they followed the rules of diffusion.
5) A different process called 'active transport' is responsible.
6) Active transport uses energy from respiration to move minerals into the root hair against the concentration gradient.

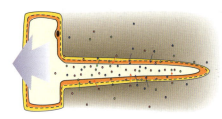

Look back at your Module B4 notes for more about diffusion and active transport.

Actively transport this information into your brain — revise...

The compensation point stuff looks pretty tricky and that graph is horrid — the important thing to remember is that the compensation point is when the amount of stuff going in and out is equal.

Module B7 — Further Biology

Humans and the Atmosphere

Plants use carbon dioxide from the atmosphere for photosynthesis.
The level of CO_2 in the atmosphere is increasing — partly due to human activity.

Human Activity Produces Lots of Carbon Dioxide

Most scientists agree that human activity is increasing the level of carbon dioxide in the Earth's atmosphere. There are several different ways we are doing this..

1) Humans release carbon dioxide into the atmosphere all the time as part of our everyday lives. Carbon dioxide is released when we burn fossil fuels. We use fossil fuels in...
   - cars and other vehicles
   - electricity production
   - industrial processes

   All of these processes cause the level of carbon dioxide in the atmosphere to increase.

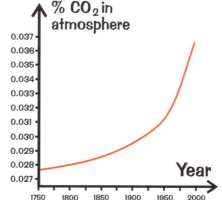

2) People around the world are also cutting down large areas of forest (deforestation) for timber and to clear land for farming and housing — and this affects the level of carbon dioxide in the atmosphere in various ways:

- Carbon dioxide is released when trees are burnt to clear land. (Carbon in wood is 'locked up' and doesn't contribute to atmospheric pollution — until it's released by burning.)
- Microorganisms feeding on bits of dead wood release CO_2 as a waste product of respiration.
- Cutting down loads of trees means that the amount of carbon dioxide removed from the atmosphere during photosynthesis is reduced.

So we're putting more CO_2 into the atmosphere than is being taken out.

Increased Carbon Dioxide May be Causing Global Warming

Increasing the level of carbon dioxide in the atmosphere seems to be having a big impact on the Earth. It's widely thought that it's causing an increase in temperature — global warming. If climate scientists are right, there are several reasons to be worried about global warming. Here's a few:

1) As the sea gets warmer, it will expand and ice might melt, causing sea levels to rise. This would be bad news for people living in low-lying places — they'd be flooded.
2) Hurricanes form over water that's warmer than 26 °C — so if there's more warm water, you would expect more hurricanes.
3) As weather patterns change, the food we grow will be affected, all over the world. Droughts in some places could force millions of people to move.

Most climate scientists agree that the Earth is getting warmer.
No one knows exactly how this will affect the planet and whether it's all our fault.

More people, more CO_2, more damage...

Us humans have created some big environmental problems for ourselves. Many people, and some governments, think we ought to start cleaning up the mess. Scientists can help, mainly in understanding the problems and suggesting solutions, but it's society as a whole that has to do something.

Module B7 — Further Biology

Biotechnology

Microorganisms like bacteria might not sound very special — but some can be really useful. They can be grown on a large scale to produce things like antibiotics and food.

Bacteria Have a Simple Structure

1) Bacteria are very small cells (about 1/100th the size of your body cells).
2) They have no nucleus. The chromosome is free in the cytoplasm.
3) Bacteria can contain plasmids — small, circular molecules of DNA, which are separate from the chromosome.

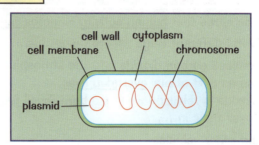

Microorganisms are Grown in Fermenters on a Large Scale

Microorganisms like bacteria and fungi can be grown in a fermenter. The fermenter gives the microorganisms the conditions they need to grow and produce their useful product. The microorganisms will need food and oxygen (if they are aerobic), and they should be kept at the right temperature.

Microorganisms Can Help Us Produce...

...Mycoprotein — Food from Fungi

1) Mycoprotein means protein from fungi. It's a type of single-celled protein. It's used to make meat substitutes for vegetarian meals — Quorn™, for example.
2) A fungus called *Fusarium* is the main source of mycoprotein. The fungus is grown in fermenters, using glucose syrup as food.
3) The fungus respires aerobically, so oxygen is supplied, plus nitrogen (as ammonia) and other minerals.

...Antibiotics Like Penicillin

Some types of bacteria and fungi can be used to produce antibiotics on a large scale. E.g. penicillin is an antibiotic made by growing *Penicillium* mould (a type of fungus) in a fermenter:

1) The mould is grown in a liquid culture medium containing sugar and other nutrients. The sugar is used up as the mould grows.
2) The mould only starts to make penicillin after using up most of the nutrients for growth.

...Enzymes for Food Manufacture

Enzymes are needed to make some types of food, e.g. cheese. To manufacture a large quantity of the food you'll need to make loads of enzyme.

1) Traditionally cheese is made using an enzyme called rennin from the lining of a calf's stomach.
2) Now rennin can be produced by genetically modified microorganisms (see next page) in a large quantity — it's used as a vegetarian substitute.

Culture medium — sounds very BBC Four to me...

Bacteria and fungi aren't always the bad guys. They can help produce delicious veggie meals, antibiotics, useful enzymes... It's not all disease and mould. Maybe they just need better PR.

Genetic Modification

Genetic modification — playing around with genes. Cool.

Genetic Modification *is* Great — Hopefully

Genetic modification is a young science with exciting possibilities (but potential dangers too). The basic idea is to move sections of DNA (genes) from one organism to another, to produce a more useful organism...

1) Microorganisms (e.g. bacteria) can be modified to produce a useful product, e.g. an enzyme or drug.
2) Plants can be modified to make them resistant to things like herbicides, frost and disease.

Genetic Modification *Involves These Important Stages*:

1) First the gene that's responsible for producing the desirable characteristic is selected.
2) It's then 'cut' from the DNA using restriction enzymes, and isolated.
3) The useful gene is often joined to a vector — a "carrier" for the gene which makes it easier to insert into a new cell. The gene is inserted into the vector using the enzyme ligase. Plasmids (see previous page) and viruses are often used as vectors.
4) The useful gene is inserted into the host DNA of the organism (usually using a vector).
5) This produces an organism with the desired characteristic.

Genetically Modified Organisms *Can be Used to Make* Insulin...

The gene for human insulin production has been put into bacteria. These are cultured in a fermenter, and the human insulin is simply extracted as they produce it. Great.
There are pros and cons to using bacteria to make drugs and hormones...

PROS
1) Using genetically modified organisms to make a substance is often relatively cheap and easy.
2) They can produce large amounts of the product.

CONS
1) If these bacteria mutated and became pathogenic (disease-causing), the foreign genes might make them more harmful and unpredictable.
2) Many people say that it's not natural to fiddle with genes.

...and *Disease-Resistant Crops*

Some plants have resistance to things like herbicides, frost damage and disease. Unfortunately, it's not always the plants we want to grow that have these features. But now, thanks to genetic modification, we can cut out the gene responsible and stick it into any useful plant we like.
There are pros and cons of genetically modifying plants...

PROS
1) GM crops can increase the yield of a crop, making more food.
2) People living in developing nations often lack nutrients in their diets. GM crops can be engineered to contain missing nutrients. For example, they're testing 'golden rice' that contains beta-carotene — lack of beta-carotene can cause blindness.

CONS
1) Not everyone is convinced that GM crops are safe. People are worried they may develop allergies to the food — although there may be no more risk for this than for eating normal foods.
2) A big concern is that transplanted genes may get out into the natural environment. For example, a herbicide-resistance gene may be picked up by weeds, creating a new 'superweed' variety.

If only there was a gene to make revision easier...

You can do great things with genetic modification. But some people worry that we don't know enough about it, or that some maniac is going to come along and combine a duck with a grapefruit. Possibly.

Module B7 — Further Biology

DNA Technology — Genetic Testing

You've already come across genetic testing before (in Module B1) so you know why genetic testing is important and the issues surrounding it. Now you need to know how genetic testing is done...

Genetic Testing Can Help Identify Genetic Disorders

There are two categories of genetic disorder that can be tested for:

1) A faulty gene — a gene that has a different sequence of bases to the normal gene.
2) A chromosome abnormality — having the wrong number of chromosomes. For example, Down syndrome is a result of having an extra copy of chromosome 21.

DNA isolated from white blood cells is often used to test for genetic disorders — it's quick and easy to take a blood sample, which contains loads of white blood cells.

Complementary DNA Can be Used to Find a Gene

IDENTIFYING A FAULTY GENE
To identify a faulty gene you can produce a gene probe. This is a strand of bases that's complementary to the faulty gene that you're looking for.

A complementary sequence contains the 'opposite' bases to the gene. Don't forget A corresponds with T, and C with G (see your Module B5 notes).

IDENTIFYING A CHROMOSOME ABNORMALITY
1) You can tell how many times a chromosome is present by trying to locate a gene that's only found on that chromosome. If this gene is present more (or less) times than usual there might be the wrong number of chromosomes.
2) A gene probe can be made to identify the gene.

USING THE GENE PROBE
The gene probe is mixed with the DNA. If the gene is present the probe will stick to it — their bases will lock together perfectly. Just like this...

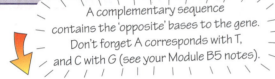

Gene Probes are Tagged so You Can Find Them

So, the gene probe can find a specific sequence of bases. But you can't see the probe with the naked eye...

1) A chemical tag is stuck on the end of the sequence of bases so you can locate the gene probe once it's stuck to a gene...
2) There are two types of tags:
   • Fluorescent — these tags will fluoresce (glow) when you shine UV light on them.
   • A radioactive chemical — can be detected using autoradiography — a bit like an X-ray.
3) If a gene is present, the chromosome it's on might look a bit like this... That funny yellow bit is where the gene probe has stuck to a gene.

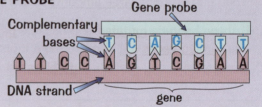

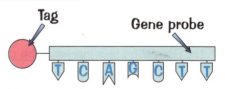

Probes won't help you with your Biology tests...

Genetic testing can be used to identify a genetic disorder in embryos and fetuses as well as in adults. When embryos are produced using IVF, they can be tested for genetic disorders before they're implanted.

Revision Summary for Module B7

This module is a mixed bag of biology fun — it's got everything. There's a bit of physiology, a dash of ecology, and a great helping of genetics... not to mention those lovely little parasites.
It's really important that you learn it all. See how well you're doing by trying to answer this terrific selection of questions.

1) What is the word equation for aerobic respiration?
2) Which molecule is directly synthesised using the energy released by respiration.
3) Anaerobic respiration releases energy. What else does it produce?
4) What type of respiration, aerobic or anaerobic, releases more energy per glucose molecule?
5) What do red blood cells carry?
6) What blood group(s) can O-type blood be given to?
7) How many alleles does the gene for blood type have?
8) What alleles could an individual of blood type A have?
9) What is meant by a double circulatory system?
10) What do valves in the heart and veins do?
11) Name the tissue that holds bones together.
12) What is the role of cartilage in joints?
13) Give one reason why it is important for health and fitness practitioners to closely monitor patients.
14) Give two reasons why a treatment programme may be modified.
15) Other than a sprain, list one common injury resulting from excessive exercise.
16) Describe one method of treating a sprain.
17) What does each bar on a pyramid of biomass represent?
18) What is the advantage of using a pyramid of biomass compared to using a pyramid of numbers?
19) What is an autotroph?
20) Give three ways energy can be lost from a trophic level.
21) Name the four main components of soil.
22) Describe the method you would use to calculate the amount of water in a soil sample.
23)*A scientist measured the percentage of water in a soil sample. The dish they used weighed 25 g, and the soil sample and the dish weighed 120 g before heating and 105 g after heating. What is the percentage water content of the soil?
24) What is commensalism?
25) Explain how specific features of the tapeworm make it suited to its environment.
26) Give two symptoms of sickle cell anaemia.
27) Explain how natural selection has resulted in an increased frequency of the sickle-cell allele in certain populations.
28) Write the word equation for photosynthesis.
29) Give three main ways plants use glucose.
30) Explain what is meant by a limiting factor.
31) Describe an experiment used to investigate the ideal conditions for a plant.
32) When do plants respire?
33) Describe what is meant by the compensation point.
34) Give one way humans are increasing the level of carbon dioxide in the atmosphere.
35) Describe how bacteria and fungi can be produced on a large scale.
36) Explain how a human gene can be transferred into bacterial DNA.
37) What is a gene probe?
38) Name the two types of gene probe tags.

Answer on page 68.

Module B7 — Further Biology

Alkanes

This module kicks off with some exciting organic chemistry, hooray. Organic chemistry is all about carbon compounds — it's good because everything is grouped into nice, tidy families. So, to begin, the alkanes...

Alkanes Are a Family of Hydrocarbons

1) Alkanes are made up of chains of carbon atoms surrounded by hydrogen atoms.
2) Alkanes only contain single covalent bonds (see your Module C5 notes).
3) The alkane family contains molecules that look similar, but have different length chains of carbon atoms.
4) All alkanes have the formula: C_nH_{2n+2} n is just the number of carbon atoms in the chain.

Methane, Ethane, Propane and Butane are Alkanes

The first four alkanes are methane, ethane, propane and butane.

Name	Methane	Ethane	Propane	Butane
Molecular formula	CH_4	C_2H_6	C_3H_8	C_4H_{10}
Structural formula	H-C-H with H above and below	H-C-C-H with Hs	H-C-C-C-H with Hs	H-C-C-C-C-H with Hs
Ball-and-stick representation				

Alkanes Burn to Give Carbon Dioxide and Water

Alkanes burn to produce carbon dioxide and water, provided there's plenty of oxygen around.

alkane + oxygen → carbon dioxide + water

You need to be able to give a balanced symbol equation for the combustion (burning) of an alkane when you're given its molecular formula. It's pretty easy — here's an example:

Make sure you end up with the same number of Cs, Hs and Os on either side of the arrow.

$CH_4(g) + 2O_2(g) \rightarrow 2H_2O(l) + CO_2(g)$

Don't forget your state symbols — s for solid, l for liquid and g for gas.

Alkanes Don't React with Most Chemicals

1) Alkanes are pretty unreactive towards most chemicals.
2) They don't react with aqueous reagents (substances dissolved in water).
3) Alkanes don't react because the C–C bonds and C–H bonds in them are unreactive.

Alkane anybody who doesn't learn this lot properly...

The clever thing about the names of alkanes is that they tell you their structure — "Meth-" means "one carbon atom", "eth-" means "two C atoms", "prop-" means "three C atoms", "but-" means "four C atoms".

Alcohols

You need to learn the structure, physical properties, chemical properties and uses of alcohols.

Alcohols Have an '-OH' Functional Group and End in '-ol'

1) The general formula for an alcohol is $C_nH_{2n+1}OH$.
2) You need to know the first two alcohols — methanol CH_3OH and ethanol C_2H_5OH.
3) The '–OH' bit is called the functional group.
4) All alcohols have similar properties because they all have the –OH functional group.

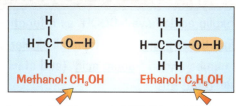

Methanol: CH_3OH Ethanol: C_2H_5OH

Don't write CH_4O instead of CH_3OH, or C_2H_6O instead of C_2H_5OH — it doesn't show the functional -OH group.

Alcohols, Alkanes and Water — The Similarities and Differences

You need to know how alcohols compare with alkanes and water in terms of their physical properties:

1) Ethanol is soluble in water. Alkanes are insoluble in water.
2) Ethanol and water are both good solvents — lots of things dissolve in them.
3) The boiling point of ethanol is 78 °C. This is lower than the boiling point of water (100 °C), but much higher than the boiling point of a similar size alkane (e.g. ethane has a boiling point of –103 °C).
4) Ethanol is a liquid at room temperature. It evaporates easily and gives off fumes (i.e. it's volatile). Methane and ethane are also volatile, but are gases at room temperature. Water is liquid at room temp, but not volatile.

Alcohols are Used as Solvents and Fuels and in Manufacturing

1) Alcohols, such as methanol and ethanol, can dissolve lots of compounds that water can't — e.g. hydrocarbons and oils. This makes methanol and ethanol very useful solvents in industry.
2) Methanol is also used in industry as a starting point for manufacturing other organic chemicals.
3) Ethanol is used in perfumes and aftershave lotions as it can mix with both the oils (which give the smell) and the water (that makes up the bulk).
4) 'Methylated spirit' (or 'meths') is ethanol with chemicals (e.g. methanol) added to it. It's used to clean paint brushes and as a fuel (among other things).
5) Alcohols burn in air because they contain hydrocarbon chains. Pure ethanol is clean burning so it is sometimes mixed with petrol and used as fuel for cars to conserve crude oil.

Alcohols React With Sodium

1) Sodium metal reacts gently with ethanol, to produce sodium ethoxide and hydrogen.

   | sodium | + | ethanol | → | sodium ethoxide | + | hydrogen |

2) Sodium metal reacts much more vigorously with water — even melting because of the heat of the reaction.

   | sodium | + | water | → | sodium hydroxide | + | hydrogen |

3) Alkanes do not react with sodium at all.

Quick tip — don't fill your car with single malt whisky...

Alcohols don't have too many chemical reactions that you need to know about for GCSE — just the two above. You do need to know the formulas, the physical properties and the uses of alcohols though. And remember — there are an awful lot more uses for alcohols than just making drinks.

Module C7 — Further Chemistry

Carboxylic Acids

Carboxylic acids are another happy family of organic chemicals.

Carboxylic Acids Have Functional Group -COOH

1) Carboxylic acids have '-COOH' as a functional group.
2) The functional group gives them all similar properties.
3) Their names end in '-anoic acid' (and start with the normal 'meth/eth...').

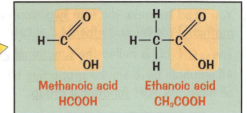

Methanoic acid HCOOH   Ethanoic acid CH_3COOH

Carboxylic Acids React Like Other Acids

1) Carboxylic acids react with alkalis, carbonates and reactive metals just like any other acid.
2) The salts formed in these reactions end in -anoate — e.g. methanoic acid forms a methanoate, ethanoic acid forms an ethanoate, etc.

Carboxylic acids react with metals to give a salt and hydrogen:

> ethanoic acid + magnesium → magnesium ethanoate + hydrogen
> $2CH_3COOH_{(aq)} + Mg_{(s)} \rightarrow Mg(CH_3CO_2)_{2(aq)} + H_{2(g)}$

Carboxylic acids react with alkalis to form a salt and water:

> ethanoic acid + magnesium hydroxide → magnesium ethanoate + water
> $2CH_3COOH_{(aq)} + Mg(OH)_{2(aq)} \rightarrow Mg(CH_3CO_2)_{2(aq)} + 2H_2O_{(l)}$

Carboxylic acids react with carbonates to give a salt, water and carbon dioxide:

> ethanoic acid + magnesium carbonate → magnesium ethanoate + water + carbon dioxide
> $2CH_3COOH_{(aq)} + MgCO_{3(aq)} \rightarrow Mg(CH_3CO_2)_{2(aq)} + H_2O_{(l)} + CO_{2(g)}$

3) Carboxylic acids are weak acids (p.33). They don't react as fast as strong acids like hydrochloric acid.

Carboxylic Acids Stink

1) Carboxylic acids often have strong smells and tastes — they're the reason your sweaty socks stink after P.E. and why gone off (rancid) butter tastes gross.
2) If wine or beer is left open to the air, the ethanol is oxidised to ethanoic acid. This is why drinking wine after it's been open for a few days is like drinking vinegar — it is vinegar.

You can also write C_2H_5OH as CH_3CH_2OH — it shows the structure more clearly.

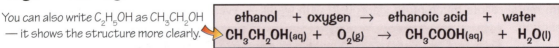

> ethanol + oxygen → ethanoic acid + water
> $CH_3CH_2OH_{(aq)} + O_{2(g)} \rightarrow CH_3COOH_{(aq)} + H_2O_{(l)}$

3) The strong smell and taste can be useful sometimes too...
Vinegar is a dilute solution of ethanoic acid and tasty on your chips.

Ethanoic acid — it's not just for putting on your chips...

The reactions of carboxylic acids are easy — they react just like any acid (and have a pH less than 7). Examiners like you to be able to give some real-world uses too. Trust me... there are worse topics.

Module C7 — Further Chemistry

Esters

Esters are lovely things — all fruity and sweet, mmm...

Esters Have Functional Group -COO-

1) <u>Esters</u> are another <u>family</u> of organic chemicals. They all have the <u>same</u> functional group, –COO–.
2) They're formed from an <u>alcohol</u> and a <u>carboxylic acid</u>. It's called an <u>esterification</u> reaction.
3) You need to know the <u>word equation</u> for the reaction:

$$\text{alcohol + carboxylic acid} \rightleftharpoons \text{ester + water}$$

An arrow like '⇌' means the reaction is <u>reversible</u> — it goes both ways. See p.33.

Esters are Often Used in Flavourings and Perfumes

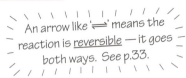

1) Many esters have <u>pleasant smells</u> — often quite <u>sweet and fruity</u>. The <u>nice fragrances</u> and <u>flavours</u> of lots of fruits come from esters.
2) They're also <u>volatile</u>. This makes them ideal for perfumes (the molecules evaporate easily, so they can drift to the smell receptors in your nose).
3) Esters are also used to make <u>flavourings</u> and <u>aromas</u> — e.g. there are esters that smell or taste of rum, apple, orange, banana, grape, pineapple, etc.
4) Some esters are used in <u>ointments</u> (they give Deep Heat its smell).
5) Other esters are used as <u>solvents</u> for paint, ink, glue and in nail varnish remover.
6) Esters are also used as <u>plasticisers</u> — they're added to plastics to make them more flexible.

Fats and Oils are Esters of Glycerol and Fatty Acids

1) Fatty acids are <u>carboxylic acids</u> with long chains. They often have between 16 and 20 carbon atoms.
2) Glycerol is an <u>alcohol</u> — notice that '-ol' at the end.
3) Fatty acids and glycerol combine to make <u>fats</u> and <u>oils</u>.
4) Most of a fat or oil molecule consists of <u>fatty acid chains</u> — these give them many of their <u>properties</u>.
5) Fatty acids can be <u>saturated</u> (only C–C single bonds) or <u>unsaturated</u> (with C=C double bonds).

Plants and Animals Make Oils and Fats to Store Energy

1) Fats have lots of <u>energy</u> packed into them — so they're good at <u>storing</u> energy.
2) When an organism has <u>more</u> energy than it needs it <u>stores</u> the extra as <u>fat</u>. The fat can then be used <u>later</u> on when the organism needs more energy.
3) The fats that plants and animals make have <u>different</u> properties:

<u>Animal fats</u> have mainly <u>saturated</u> hydrocarbon chains. They contain very <u>few</u> C=C bonds. They are normally <u>solid</u> at room temperature.

<u>Vegetable oils</u> have mainly <u>unsaturated</u> hydrocarbon chains. They contain <u>lots</u> of C=C bonds. They are normally <u>liquid</u> at room temperature.

What's a chemist's favourite chocolate — ester eggs...

If you want to impress your friends learn the full name of glycerol — propane-1,2,3-triol — then just casually drop it into conversation, as in "On Saturday I... err..." well, good luck with that one.

Module C7 — Further Chemistry

Making an Ester

Take an alcohol from p.27, mix it with an acid from p.28, and what have you got... an ester, that's what.

How to Make an Ester — Reflux, Distil, Purify, Dry

Making esters is a little more complicated than just mixing an alcohol and a carboxylic acid together. The reaction is reversible so some of the ester formed will react with the water produced and re-form the carboxylic acid and alcohol. To get a pure ester you need a multi-step reaction and purification procedure.

1) Refluxing — The Reaction

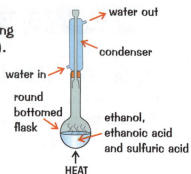

To make ethyl ethanoate you need to react ethanol with ethanoic acid, using a catalyst to speed things up (concentrated sulfuric acid is a good choice).

Heating the mixture also speeds up the reaction — but you can't just stick a Bunsen under it as the ethanol will evaporate or catch fire before it can react.

Instead, the mixture's gently heated in a flask fitted with a condenser — this catches the vapours and recycles them back into the flask, giving them time to react. This handy method is called refluxing.

2) Distillation

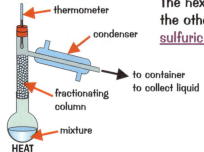

The next step is distillation. This separates your lovely ester from all the other stuff left in the flask (unreacted alcohol and carboxylic acid, sulfuric acid and water).

The mixture's heated below a fractionating column. As it starts to boil, the vapour goes up the fractionating column.

When the temperature at the top of the column reaches the boiling point of ethyl ethanoate, the liquid that flows out of the condenser is collected. This liquid is impure ethyl ethanoate.

3) Purification

The liquid collected (the distillate) is poured into a tap funnel and then treated to remove its impurities, as follows:

The mixture is shaken with sodium carbonate solution to remove acidic impurities. Ethyl ethanoate doesn't mix with water, so the mixture separates into two layers, and the lower layer can be tapped off (removed).

The remaining upper layer is then shaken with concentrated calcium chloride solution to remove any ethanol. Again, the lower layer can be tapped off and removed.

4) Drying

Any remaining water in the ethyl ethanoate can be removed by shaking it with lumps of anhydrous calcium chloride, which absorb the water — this is called drying. Finally, the pure ethyl ethanoate can be separated from the solid calcium chloride by filtration.

Esterification — it's 'esterical stuff...

Sorry about that, it's a little bit tricky really. The secret is to get your head around each step of the process before you try and put it all together. Read each step, cover, scribble... you know the drill.

Energy Transfer in Reactions

Whenever chemical reactions occur, there are changes in energy. This is kind of interesting if you think of the number of chemical reactions that are involved in everyday life.

Reactions are Exothermic or Endothermic

An **EXOTHERMIC reaction** is one which gives out energy to the surroundings, usually in the form of heat and usually shown by a rise in temperature.

E.g. fuels burning or neutralisation reactions.

An **ENDOTHERMIC reaction** is one which takes in energy from the surroundings, usually in the form of heat and usually shown by a fall in temperature.

E.g. photosynthesis.

Energy Level Diagrams Show if it's Exo- or Endothermic

In exothermic reactions ΔH is –ve

1) This shows an exothermic reaction — the products are at a lower energy than the reactants.
2) The difference in height represents the energy given out in the reaction. ΔH is –ve here.

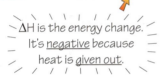
ΔH is the energy change. It's negative because heat is given out.

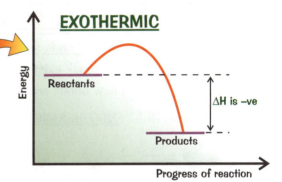

In endothermic reactions ΔH is +ve

1) This shows an endothermic reaction because the products are at a higher energy than the reactants, so ΔH is +ve.
2) The difference in height represents the energy taken in during the reaction.

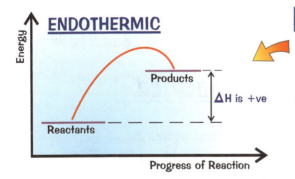

Activation Energy is the Energy Needed to Start a Reaction

1) The activation energy is the minimum amount of energy needed for a reaction to happen.
2) It's a bit like having to climb up one side of a hill before you can ski/snowboard/sledge/fall down the other side.
3) If the energy input is less than the activation energy there won't be enough energy to start the reaction — so nothing will happen.

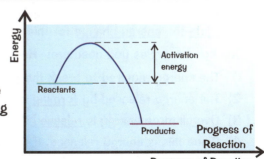

Right, so burning gives out heat — really...

This whole energy transfer thing is a fairly simple idea — don't be put off by the long words. Remember, "exo-" = exit, "-thermic" = heat, so an exothermic reaction is one that gives out heat. And "endo-" = erm... the other one. Okay, so there's no easy way to remember that one. Tough.

Module C7 — Further Chemistry

Catalysts and Bond Energies

Energy transfer in chemical reactions is all to do with making and breaking bonds.

Catalysts Lower the Activation Energy

1) A catalyst is a substance which changes the speed of a reaction, without being changed or used up in the reaction.
2) Catalysts lower the activation energy needed for reactions to happen by providing alternative routes.
3) The effect of a catalyst is shown by the lower curve on the diagram.
4) The overall energy change for the reaction, ΔH, remains the same though.

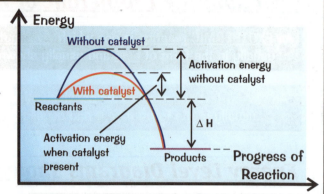

Energy Must Always be Supplied to Break Bonds

1) During a chemical reaction, old bonds are broken and new bonds are formed.
2) Energy must be supplied to break existing bonds — so bond breaking is an endothermic process.
3) Energy is released when new bonds are formed — so bond formation is an exothermic process.

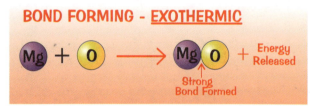

In exothermic reactions the energy released by forming bonds is greater than the energy used to break them.
In endothermic reactions the energy used to break bonds is greater than the energy released by forming them.

Bond Energy Calculations — Need to be Practised

1) Every chemical bond has a particular bond energy associated with it.
   This bond energy varies slightly depending on the compound the bond occurs in.
2) You can use these known bond energies to calculate the overall energy change for a reaction.
   You need to practise a few of these, but the basic idea is really very simple...

Example: The Formation of HCl

Using known bond energies you can calculate the energy change for this reaction:

$$H-H + Cl-Cl \longrightarrow \begin{matrix} H-Cl \\ H-Cl \end{matrix}$$

The bond energies you need are: H—H: +436 kJ;   Cl—Cl: +242 kJ;   H—Cl: +431 kJ.

1) The energy required to break the original bonds is 436 + 242 = +678 kJ
2) The energy released by forming the new bonds is 2 × 431 = +862 kJ
3) Overall more energy is released than is used to form the products: 862 − 678 = 184 kJ released.
4) Since this is energy released, if you wanted to show ΔH you'd need to put a negative sign in front of it to indicate that it's an exothermic reaction, like this: ΔH = −184 kJ

Energy transfer — make sure you take it all in...

Bond energies don't tell you the amount of energy associated with a single bond. They tell you the amount of energy associated with 6×10^{23} bonds. This might seem a little bit odd, but it makes sense to the clever chemistry types. In the exam you'll be given all the bond energies you'll need to use.

Module C7 — Further Chemistry

Reversible Reactions

A <u>reversible reaction</u> is one where the <u>products</u> of the reaction can react with each other and <u>convert back</u> to the original reactants. In other words, <u>it can go both ways</u>.

> A <u>reversible reaction</u> is one where the <u>products</u> of the reaction can <u>themselves react</u> to produce the <u>original reactants</u>.
>
> A + B ⇌ C + D
>
> This is the symbol for a reversible reaction.

Reversible Reactions Will Reach Dynamic Equilibrium

1) If a reversible reaction takes place in a <u>closed system</u> then a state of <u>equilibrium</u> will always be reached. (A '<u>closed system</u>' just means that none of the reactants or products can <u>escape</u>.)

2) <u>Equilibrium</u> means that the <u>relative (%) quantities</u> of reactants and products will reach a certain <u>balance</u> and stay there.

3) It is in fact a <u>dynamic equilibrium</u>, which means that the reactions are still taking place in <u>both directions</u>, but the <u>overall effect is nil</u> because the forward and reverse reactions <u>cancel</u> each other out. The reactions are taking place at <u>exactly the same rate</u> in both directions.

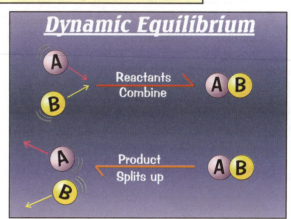

Dynamic Equilibrium

Ionisation of Weak Acids is a Reversible Reaction

When acids are dissolved in water they <u>ionise</u> — they release <u>hydrogen ions</u>, H^+. This is what makes them acidic. For example,

An H^+ ion is just a proton.

$$HCl_{(aq)} \rightarrow H^+_{(aq)} + Cl^-_{(aq)}$$
$$H_2SO_{4(aq)} \rightarrow 2H^+_{(aq)} + SO_4^{2-}_{(aq)}$$

There's more about acids back in Module C6 — check your notes.

Acids either ionise <u>completely</u> or reach a <u>dynamic equilibrium</u> — it all depends on the <u>type</u> of acid.

1) <u>Strong acids</u> (e.g. hydrochloric acid) <u>ionise almost completely</u> in water. This means almost <u>every</u> hydrogen is <u>released</u> — so there are <u>loads</u> of H^+ ions.

2) <u>Weak acids</u> (e.g. carboxylic acids) ionise only very <u>slightly</u>. Only <u>some</u> of the hydrogens in the compound are released — so only <u>small numbers</u> of H^+ ions are formed. For example,

> <u>Strong acid</u>: $HCl_{(aq)} \longrightarrow H^+_{(aq)} + Cl^-_{(aq)}$
>
> <u>Weak acid</u>: $CH_3COOH_{(aq)} \rightleftharpoons H^+_{(aq)} + CH_3COO^-_{(aq)}$

Use a 'reversible reaction' arrow for a weak acid.

3) The ionisation of a <u>weak</u> acid is a <u>reversible reaction</u>. Since only a few H^+ ions are released, the <u>equilibrium</u> is well to the <u>left</u> (i.e. there's a lot more CH_3COOH molecules in the solution than there are H^+ and CH_3COO^- ions).

Keep going back and forth over reversible reactions...

...and they'll soon make sense. Acids are <u>acidic</u> because of H^+ ions. <u>Strong</u> acids are strong because they let go of <u>all</u> their H^+ ions at the drop of a hat... well, at the drop of a drop of water. This is tricky, it's true, but if you can get your head round this, then you can probably cope with just about anything.

Module C7 — Further Chemistry

Analytical Procedures

The next few pages are all about finding out exactly what is contained in a mystery substance.

Qualitative Analysis Tells You What a Sample Contains

1) Qualitative analysis tells you which substances are present in a sample.
2) It doesn't tell you how much of each substance there is — that's where quantitative analysis comes in.

Quantitative Analysis Tells You How Much it Contains

1) Quantitative analysis tells you how much of a substance is present in a sample.
2) It can be used to work out the molecular formula of the sample. E.g. if you had a sample containing carbon and hydrogen you'd know it was a hydrocarbon, but without quantitative analysis, you won't know if it's methane, butane or even 3,4-dimethylheptane...

Chemical Analysis is Carried Out On Samples

1) You usually analyse just a sample of the material under test. There's quite a few reasons for this.
2) It might be very difficult to test all of the material if you've got an awful lot of it — or you might want to just test a small bit so that you can use the rest for something else.

3) Taking a sample also means that if something goes wrong with the test, you can go back for another sample and try again.
4) A sample must represent the bulk of the material being tested — it wouldn't tell you anything very useful if it didn't.

Samples are Analysed in Solution

Samples are usually tested in solution. A solution is made by dissolving the sample in a solvent. There are two types of solution — aqueous and non-aqueous. Which type of solution you use depends on the type of substance you're testing.

| An aqueous solution means the solvent is water. They're shown by the state symbol (aq). | A non-aqueous solution means the solvent is anything other than water — e.g. ethanol. |

Standard Procedures Mean Everyone Does Things the Same Way

Whether testing chemicals or measuring giraffes, scientists follow 'standard procedures' — clear instructions describing exactly how to carry out these practical tasks.

1) Standard procedures are agreed methods of working — they are chosen because they're the safest, most effective and most accurate methods to use.
2) Standard procedures can be agreed within a company, nationally, or internationally.
3) They're useful because wherever and whenever a test is done, the result should always be the same — it should give reliable results every time.
4) There are standard procedures for the collection and storage of a sample, as well as how it should be analysed.

Analysis — don't they do that on Match of the Day?...

If you're trying to detect a certain substance in a sample, then there has to be a reasonable amount of the stuff you're looking for. You'd stand no chance of finding one molecule in a great big cake.

Module C7 — Further Chemistry

Analysis — Chromatography

Chromatography is one analysis method that you need to know inside out and upside down... read on.

Chromatography uses Two Phases

Chromatography is an analysis method that's used to separate the substances in a mixture.
You can then use it to identify the individual substances.
There are lots of different types of chromatography — but they all have two 'phases':

- A mobile phase — where the molecules can move. This is always a liquid or a gas.
- A stationary phase — where the molecules can't move. This can be a solid or a really thick liquid.

1) The components in the mixture separate out as the mobile phase moves across the stationary phase.
2) How quickly a chemical moves depends on how it "distributes" itself between the two phases — this is why different chemicals separate out and end up at different points (see below).
3) The molecules of each chemical constantly move between the mobile and the stationary phases.
4) They are said to reach a "dynamic equilibrium" — at equilibrium the amount leaving the stationary phase for the mobile phase is the same as the amount leaving the mobile phase for the stationary phase. But be careful, this doesn't (necessarily) mean there is the same amount of chemical in each phase.

In Paper Chromatography the Stationary Phase is Paper

1) In paper chromatography, a spot of the substance being tested is put onto a baseline on the paper.
2) The bottom of the paper is placed in a beaker containing a solvent, such as ethanol or water. The solvent is the mobile phase.
3) The stationary phase is the chromatography paper (often filter paper).

Here's what happens:

1) The solvent moves up the paper.
2) The chemicals in the sample dissolve in the solvent and move between it and the paper. This sets up an equilibrium between the solvent and the paper.
3) When they're in the mobile phase the chemicals move up the paper with the solvent.
4) Before the solvent reaches the top of the paper, the paper is removed from the beaker.
5) The different chemicals in the sample form separate spots on the paper. The chemicals that spend more time in the mobile phase than the stationary phase form spots further up the paper.

The amount of time the molecules spend in each phase depends on two things:
- how soluble they are in the solvent,
- how attracted they are to the paper.

So molecules with a higher solubility in the solvent, and which are less attracted to the paper, will spend more time in the mobile phase — and they'll be carried further up the paper.

Thin-Layer Chromatography has a Different Stationary Phase

1) Thin-layer chromatography (TLC) is very similar to paper chromatography, but the stationary phase is a thin layer of solid — e.g. silica gel spread onto a glass plate.
2) The mobile phase is a solvent such as ethanol (just like in paper chromatography).

Learning about this — it's just a phase you go through...

The tricky thing about understanding how chromatography works is that you can't see the chemicals moving between the two phases — you'll just have to believe that it does happen.

Module C7 — Further Chemistry

Analysis — Chromatography

You can Calculate the R_f Value for Each Chemical

1) The result of chromatography analysis is called a chromatogram.
2) Some of the spots on the chromatogram might be colourless. If they are, you need to use a locating agent to show where they are, e.g. you might have to spray the chromatogram with a reagent.
3) You need to know how to work out the R_f values for spots (solutes) on a chromatogram.
   An R_f value is the ratio between the distance travelled by the dissolved substance and the distance travelled by the solvent. You can find them using the formula:

$$R_f = \frac{\text{distance travelled by substance}}{\text{distance travelled by solvent}}$$

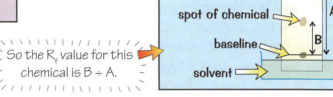

So the R_f value for this chemical is B ÷ A.

4) Chromatography is often carried out to see if a certain substance is present in a mixture. You run a pure, known sample of the substance alongside the unknown mixture. If the R_f values match, the substances may be the same (although it doesn't definitely prove they are the same).
5) Chemists use substances called standard reference materials (SRMs) to check the identities of substances. These have carefully controlled concentrations and purities.

Gas Chromatography is a Bit More High-Tech

Gas chromatography (GC) is used to analyse unknown substances too. If they're not already gases, then they have to be vaporised.

- The mobile phase is an unreactive gas such as nitrogen.
- The stationary phase is a viscous (thick) liquid, such as an oil.

The process is quite different from paper chromatography and TLC:
1) The unknown mixture is injected into a long tube coated on the inside with the stationary phase.
2) The mixture moves along the tube with the mobile phase until it comes out the other end. Like in the other chromatography methods, the substances are distributed between the phases.
3) The time it takes a chemical to travel through the tube is called the retention time.
4) The retention time is different for each chemical — it's what's used to identify it.

The chromatogram from gas chromatography is a graph. Each peak on the graph represents a different chemical.

- The distance along the x-axis is the retention time — which can be looked up to find out what the chemical is.
- The area under the peak shows you how much of that chemical was in the sample.

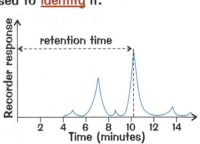

Comb-atography — identifies mysterious things in your hair...

Chromatography works by showing how mystery chemicals get distributed between mobile and stationary phases — that's what the R_f value represents. All chemicals get distributed differently, so that's how you can tell which is which. It's great — all you need is some paper and a bit of solvent.

Analysis — Solution Concentrations

A rather dull and boring page I'm afraid. But at least there are some calculations on it. Yay.

Concentration = Mass ÷ Volume

The concentration of a solution is measured in grams per dm^3 (i.e. grams per litre — one dm^3 is a litre). So 1 gram of stuff in 1 dm^3 of solution has a concentration of 1 gram per dm^3 (or 1 g/dm^3).

There's a nice formula to work out the concentration of a solution:

concentration = mass of solute ÷ volume of solution

Concentration (in g/dm^3) — Mass (in g) — Volume (in dm^3)

Make sure you know how to use it — you might need to rearrange it:

Example 1: 25 g of copper sulfate is dissolved in 500 cm^3 of water. What's the concentration in g/dm^3?

Answer: Make sure the amounts are in the right units — mass in g and volume in dm^3.
Substitute the values into the formula: concentration = 25 g ÷ 0.5 dm^3 = **50 g/dm^3**

Convert the volume to dm^3 by dividing by 1000.

Example 2: What mass of sodium chloride is in 300 cm^3 of solution with a concentration of 12 g/dm^3?

Answer: Rearrange the formula using the triangle: mass = concentration × volume.
Substitute the values into the formula: mass = 12 g/dm^3 × 0.3 dm^3 = **3.6 g**

A Standard Solution Has a Known Concentration

A standard solution is any solution that you know the concentration of.
Making a standard solution needs careful measuring and a hint of maths:

Example: Make 250 cm^3 of a 314 g/dm^3 solution of sodium chloride.

1) First work out how many grams of solute you need by using the formula: mass = concentration × volume
   = 314 g/dm^3 × 0.25 dm^3 = 78.5 g

   Remember — convert cm^3 to dm^3

2) Carefully weigh out this mass of solute — first weigh the beaker, note the weight, then add the correct mass.

3) Add a small amount of distilled water to the beaker and stir until all the solute has dissolved.

4) Tip the solution into a volumetric flask — make sure it's the right size for the volume you're making. Use a funnel to make sure it all goes in.

5) Rinse the beaker and stirring rod with distilled water and add that to the flask too. This makes sure there's no solute clinging to the beaker or rod.

6) Now top the flask up to the correct volume (250 cm^3) with more distilled water. Make sure the bottom of the meniscus reaches the line — when you get close to the line use a pipette to add water drop by drop. If you go over the line you'll have to start all over again.

7) Stopper the bottle and turn it upside down a few times to make sure it's all mixed.

8) Check the meniscus again and add a drop or two of water if you need to.

Wondering what's on telly? — no, don't lose concentration...

A high concentration is like a rugby team in a mini. Or everyone in Britain living on the Isle of Wight.
A low concentration is like a guy stranded on a desert island, or a small fish in a big lake. Poetic, no?

Module C7 — Further Chemistry

Analysis — Titration

You saw the basics of titrations in Module C6. Here's a bit more that you need to know about them though.

You Need Several Consistent Readings

In a titration, you record the volume of acid (or alkali) added from a burette to neutralise the alkali (or acid). Sometimes you get a weird result (called an anomalous result) — this might be caused by faulty equipment, or human error (perhaps the scale was read incorrectly) — so it's best to repeat the titration a few times. If your values are all very similar you can be confident your results are reliable. If they're more spread out, you can't be so certain of what the 'true' result should be.

- The first titration should be a rough titration to get an approximate idea of the end-point.
- You then need to repeat the whole thing carefully a few times, making sure you get (pretty much) the same answer each time (within about 0.2 cm^3).
- A mean (average) value can then be calculated from the repeats — but ignore any anomalous results.

> **EXAMPLE** A titration was repeated four times. This table shows the results:
>
> The second result is very different from the others — it's anomalous. But the other three results are close together. You can be pretty confident that the actual result lies close to 22.3 and 22.4 cm^3.
>
> | Titration | 1 | 2 | 3 | 4 |
> |---|---|---|---|---|
> | Volume added (cm^3) | 22.3 | 30.0 | 22.4 | 22.3 |
>
> Work out the mean of the results that are close together and use it for any later calculations or graphs.
> mean volume = (22.3 + 22.4 + 22.3) ÷ 3 = 22.33 cm^3 (to 2 d.p.)

Interpreting the Results of a Titration

Titrations are also used to measure purity.

You can use titrations to work out the identity of unknown element in a compound...

> **Example**
>
> 25 cm^3 of an unknown metal hydroxide solution (MOH) with a concentration of 192 g/dm^3 has been titrated with 40 cm^3 of hydrochloric acid solution with a concentration of 182.5 g/dm^3.
> Here's the equation for the reaction: HCl + MOH → MCl + H$_2$O
> Determine what the metal hydroxide is. (Relative atomic masses: H = 1, O = 16, Cl = 35.5)

You want to find out the relative formula mass for MOH, so you can figure out what M stands for.

Step 1: First find out the mass of acid and the mass of alkali that react.

There are 192 g of MOH in each dm^3. So in 0.025 dm^3 (25 cm^3 ÷ 1000) there is 0.025 × 192 = **4.8 g of MOH**.
There's 182.5 g of HCl in each dm^3. So in 0.04 dm^3, there is 0.04 × 182.5 = **7.3 g of HCl**.

Step 2: Find the relative formula mass of the known solute. M$_r$ of HCl = 1 + 35.5 = 36.5.

Step 3: Find the relative formula mass of the unknown solute using the balanced equation.

From the equation, you know that 1 molecule of HCl reacts with 1 molecule of MOH.
And you know that 7.3 g of HCl reacts with 4.8 g of MOH.
The relative formula masses tell you how the mass of the molecules of HCl and MOH compare to each other. So you can use this formula to find the relative formula mass (M$_r$) of MOH:

> mass of HCl ÷ M$_r$ of HCl = mass of MOH ÷ M$_r$ of MOH

7.3 ÷ 36.5 = 4.8 ÷ M$_r$ of MOH ⇒ M$_r$ of MOH = **24**

Step 4: Identify the metal hydroxide. M$_r$ of MOH = (A$_r$ of M) + 16 + 1 = 24, so A$_r$ of M = 7.
Lithium has a relative atomic mass of 7, so the metal hydroxide, MOH, is **lithium hydroxide, LiOH**.

More numbers? — might as well be doing maths... urrgh...

In titration calculations, look at the information you're given, and see what you can work out with it.

The Chemical Industry

Absolutely loads of some types of chemicals are used — such as fertilisers. Well they don't just grow on trees. No, they have to be made. And made they are — on a massive scale.

Some Chemicals are Produced on a Large Scale...

There are certain chemicals that industries need thousands and thousands of tonnes of every year — ammonia, sulfuric acid, sodium hydroxide and phosphoric acid are four examples you should know. Chemicals like these that are produced on a large scale are called bulk chemicals.

...And Some are Produced on a Small Scale

Some chemicals aren't needed in such large amounts — but that doesn't mean they're any less important.

Chemicals produced on a smaller scale are called fine chemicals. Some examples to learn are drugs, food additives and fragrances.

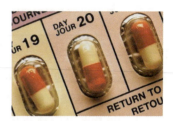

New Chemical Products Need Lots of Research

Before new chemical products are made, a huge amount of research and development work goes on. This can take years, and be really expensive, but it's worth it in the end if the company makes lots of money out of the new product.

For example, to make a new product efficiently a new catalyst might have to be found. This is likely to involve:

1) Testing potential catalysts using a process of trial and error.
2) Making computer models of the reaction to try to work out which substance might work as a catalyst.
3) Designing or refining the manufacture of the catalyst to make sure that the new product can be mass-produced safely, efficiently, and cost effectively.
4) Investigating the risks to the environment of using the new catalyst and trying to minimise them.
5) Monitoring the quality of the product to make sure that it is not affected by the catalyst.

These jobs, and lots of other types of work, are done by people in the chemical industry. You don't need to know about all of them off-by-heart, but you do need to be able to interpret information about them.

Government Regulations Protect People and the Environment

Governments place strict controls on everything to do with chemical processes. This is done to protect workers, the general public and the environment. For example, there are regulations about...

1) Using chemicals — e.g. sulfuric acid is sprayed on potato fields to destroy the leaves and stalks of the potato plants and make harvesting easier. Government regulations restrict how much acid can be used and require signs to be displayed to warn the public.
2) Storage — many dangerous chemicals have to be stored in locked storerooms. Noxious (poisonous) chemicals must be stored in either sealed containers or well-ventilated store cupboards.
3) Transport — e.g. lorries transporting chemicals must display hazard symbols and identification numbers to help the emergency services deal safely with any accidents and spills.

Fine chemicals — by appointment to Her Majesty, The Queen...

Producing bulk chemicals is like painting a house — it's huge, so you slap that paint on with a great big brush. Producing fine chemicals is like painting a picture — much smaller and more fiddly. Got it?

Module C7 — Further Chemistry

Producing Chemicals

Producing chemicals is a complicated business. Luckily most processes involve the same stages.

There Are Several Stages Involved in Producing Chemicals

The process of producing a useful chemical from the raw materials can be split into five stages:

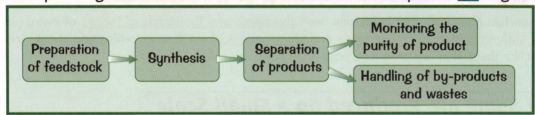

1) Raw Materials Are Converted Into Feedstocks

1) Raw materials are the naturally occurring substances which are needed, e.g. crude oil, natural gas.
2) Feedstocks are the actual reactants needed for the process, e.g. hydrogen, ethanol.
3) The raw materials usually have to be purified or changed in some way to make the feedstock.

2) Synthesis

The feedstocks (reactants) are converted by the magic of chemistry into products. The conditions have to be carefully controlled to make sure the reaction happens, and at a sensible rate.

3) The Products are Separated

1) Chemical reactions usually produce the substance you want and some other chemicals known as by-products. The by-products might be useful, or they might be waste.
2) You might also have some left-over reactants.
3) Everything has to be separated out so it can be dealt with in different ways.

4) The Purity of the Product is Monitored

1) Even after the best efforts are made to separate the product from everything else, it sometimes still has other things mixed in with it — it's not completely pure.
2) The purity of the product has to be monitored to make sure it's between certain levels.
3) Different industries need different levels of purity depending on what the product is used for. If a slightly impure product will do the job it's meant for, there's no point wasting money on purification.

5) By-products and Waste are Dealt With

1) Where possible, by-products are sold or used in another reaction.
2) If the reaction is exothermic, there may be waste heat. Heat exchangers can use excess heat to produce steam or hot water for other reactions — saving energy and money.
3) Waste products have to be carefully disposed of so they don't harm people or the environment — there are legal requirements about this.

Feedsock — when you spill your dinner over your feet...

As you might have noticed, producing chemicals isn't the most exciting of topics — but it is important. The chemical industry in Britain alone is worth billions of pounds... which makes it a lot more interesting.

Module C7 — Further Chemistry

Producing Chemicals

It'd be great if all industrial reactions were sustainable — humans could go on and on making whatever they wanted forever and ever. Life isn't like that though — so it's important to think about sustainability.

There Are Eight Key Questions About Sustainability

Sustainable processes are ones that meet people's needs today without affecting the ability of future generations to meet their own needs. Lots of factors affect whether a chemical process is sustainable.

1) WILL THE RAW MATERIALS RUN OUT?

It's great if your feedstock is renewable — you can keep on using as much as you like. The trouble is, if it's not renewable it's going to run out. And this could mean big problems for future generations.

2) HOW GOOD IS THE ATOM ECONOMY?

The atom economy of a reaction tells you how much of the mass of the reactants ends up as useful products. Pretty obviously, if you're making lots of waste, that's a problem — it all has to go somewhere. Reactions with low atom economy use up resources very quickly too.

3) WHAT DO I DO WITH THE WASTE PRODUCTS?

Waste products can be expensive to remove and dispose of responsibly. They're likely to take up space and cause pollution. One way around the problem is to find a use for the waste products rather than just throwing them away. Alternatively, there's often more than one way to make the product you want, so you try to choose a reaction that gives useful by-products.

4) WHAT ARE THE ENERGY COSTS?

If a reaction needs a lot of energy it'll be very expensive. And making energy often involves burning fossil fuels — which of course is no good for the environment. But if a process gives out energy there might be a way to use that energy for something else — saving money and the environment.

5) WILL IT DAMAGE THE ENVIRONMENT?

Clearly if the reaction produces harmful chemicals it's not going to do any good for the environment. But you need to consider where the raw materials come from too (mining, for example, can make a right mess of the countryside), and also whether the reactants or products need transporting.

6) WHAT ARE THE HEALTH AND SAFETY RISKS?

There's no doubt about it — chemistry can be dangerous. There are laws in place that companies must follow to make sure their workers and the public are not put in harm's way. Companies also have to test their products to make sure they're safe to use.

7) ARE THERE ANY BENEFITS OR RISKS TO SOCIETY?

A factory creates jobs for the local community and brings money into the area. But it may be unsightly and potentially hazardous.

8) IS IT PROFITABLE?

This is the big question for most companies — businesses are out to make money after all. If the costs of a process are higher than the income from it, then it won't be profitable.

Enough with the questions — I confess...

You could get asked about any industrial reaction in the exam. Don't panic — whatever example they give you, the same stuff applies. The trick is to use the information they give you to answer the eight key questions — the next couple of pages go through a nice big case study all about ethanol.

Module C7 — Further Chemistry

Making Ethanol

Ethanol is the alcohol people drink — but as you saw on page 27 this is far from its only use. It's also used as a fuel, a solvent and as a feedstock for other processes.

Ethanol can be Made by Fermentation

The ethanol in alcoholic drinks is usually made using fermentation.

1) Fermentation uses yeast to convert sugars into ethanol. Carbon dioxide is also produced.

$$\text{sugar} \xrightarrow{\text{yeast}} \text{ethanol} + \text{carbon dioxide}$$

Enzymes are naturally occurring catalysts.

2) The yeast cells contain zymase, an enzyme which is important in fermentation.
3) Fermentation happens fastest at about 30 °C. That's because zymase works best at this temperature. At lower temperatures, the reaction slows down. And if it's too hot the zymase is destroyed.
4) Zymase also works best at a pH of about 4 — a strongly acidic or alkaline solution will stop it working.
5) It's important to prevent oxygen getting to the fermentation process. Oxygen converts the ethanol to ethanoic acid (the acid in vinegar), which lowers the pH and can stop the enzyme working.
6) When the concentration of ethanol reaches about 10 to 20%, the fermentation reaction stops, because the yeast gets killed off by the ethanol.

Ethanol Solution can be Concentrated by Distillation

The fermented mixture can be distilled to produce more concentrated ethanol — e.g. brandy is distilled from wine, whisky is distilled from fermented grain.

1) The ethanol solution is put in a flask below a fractionating column, as shown.
2) The solution is heated so that the ethanol boils. The ethanol vapour travels up the column, cooling down as it goes.
3) The temperature is such that anything with a higher boiling point than ethanol (like water) cools to a liquid and flows back into the solution at the bottom.
4) This means that only pure ethanol vapour reaches the top of the column.
5) The ethanol vapour flows through a condenser — where it's cooled to a liquid, which is then collected.

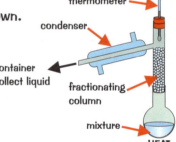

Is Fermentation A Sustainable Process?

You may get a question about the sustainability of ethanol production. The question will give you some information — your job is to interpret the data to evaluate whether the method described is sustainable.

1) Will the raw materials run out? — Sugar beet and yeast grow quickly so won't run out.
2) How good is the atom economy? — The waste CO_2 produced means it has a low atom economy. And because the enzyme is killed off by the ethanol produced, the reaction is even less efficient.
3) What do I do with my waste products? — The waste CO_2 can be released without any processing.
4) What are the energy costs? — Energy is needed to keep the reaction at its optimum temperature.
5) Will it damage the environment? — Carbon dioxide is a greenhouse gas so adds to global warming.
6) What are the health and safety risks? — The chemicals and processes do not have any specific dangers.
7) Are there any benefits or risks to society? — Making ethanol doesn't impact society (drinking it does).
8) Is it profitable? — This depends on what the ethanol is used for, e.g. drinking or fuel.

Excessive drinking — when a tipple becomes a topple...

People have been making alcohol for thousands of years. It could explain why there are so many ancient ruins all over the place — maybe the Romans were always too drunk to finish the job properly...

Module C7 — Further Chemistry

Making Ethanol

Ethanol can be Made From Biomass

Scientists have recently developed a way to make ethanol from waste biomass.
1) Waste biomass is the parts of a plant that would normally be thrown away — e.g. corn stalks, rice husks, wood pulp and straw.
2) Waste biomass cannot be fermented in the normal way because it contains a lot of cellulose. Yeast can easily convert some sugars to ethanol, but it can't convert cellulose to ethanol.
3) E. coli bacteria can be genetically modified so they can convert cellulose in waste biomass into ethanol.
4) The optimum conditions for this process are a temperature of 35 °C and a slightly acidic solution, pH 6.

Is Producing Ethanol from Biomass a Sustainable Process?

The sustainability of the biomass method is very similar to the sustainability of the standard fermentation method because they both use similar processes. The advantage of using biomass is that you don't have to grow crops specially for producing ethanol — you can use the waste from other crops.

Ethene Can be Reacted with Steam to Produce Ethanol

Fermentation is too slow for making ethanol on a large scale. Instead, ethanol is made on an industrial scale using ethane. This method allows high quality ethanol to be produced continuously and quickly.
1) Ethane is one of the hydrocarbons found in crude oil.
2) It is 'cracked' (split) to form ethene (C_2H_4) and hydrogen gas.   →   ethane → ethene + hydrogen
3) Ethene will react with steam (H_2O) to make ethanol.   →   ethene + steam → ethanol
4) The reaction needs a temperature of 300 °C and a pressure of 70 atmospheres. Phosphoric acid is used as a catalyst.

Is Producing Ethanol from Ethane a Sustainable Process?

If you get a question about sustainability it'll probably give you some information to help you. But make sure you learn about the processes too, as it won't give you all the answers.
1) Will the raw materials run out? — Crude oil is the raw material and it's non-renewable so it will run out.
2) How good is the atom economy? — Cracking ethane has a fairly high atom economy as the only waste product is hydrogen. Reacting ethene has an even higher atom economy as ethanol is the only product.
3) What do I do with my waste products? — The only waste is the hydrogen gas produced by cracking ethane. It can be reused to make ammonia in the Haber process.
4) What are the energy costs? — Energy is needed to maintain the high temperature and pressure used.
5) Will it damage the environment? — The reactions involved do not produce any waste products that directly harm the environment. But, crude oil can harm the environment, e.g. through oil spills.
6) What are the health and safety risks? — The high temperature and pressure used to produce the ethanol have to carefully controlled — otherwise it could be very dangerous.
7) Are there any benefits or risks to society? — This method has no specific impact on society.
8) Is it profitable? — Yes, manufacturing ethanol from ethene and steam is continuous and quick and the raw materials are fairly cheap — but it won't stay that way once crude oil starts to run out.

Sustainability — you're doing pretty well... just one page left...

It's important to think about the sustainability of chemical processes — it'd be rather selfish to use up all the raw materials, and leave future generations with big piles of our waste to put up with instead.

Module C7 — Further Chemistry

Revision Summary for Module C7

The end of another beautiful section — it brings a tear to my eye. Here's a handy pocket-size checklist of things to make sure you've learnt: 1. definitions — learn what all the words mean, yes even the really long ones, 2. formulas — you'll lose easy marks on calculations if you don't, 3. examples — examiners love giving you marks for dropping the odd example in here and there, 4. reactions — these are the bread and butter of chemistry, you've just gotta learn them, 5. how to do things — diagrams often help here...
I can't think of anything else right now, so try these questions to check I haven't forgotten anything vital.

1) What is the general formula for an alkane?
2) Write a balanced equation for the combustion of ethane in plenty of oxygen.
3) How does the reaction of sodium with ethanol differ from the reaction of sodium with water?
4) What is the functional group of carboxylic acids?
5) Write a balanced equation for the reaction of ethanoic acid and calcium.
6) Describe in detail how you could prepare a pure sample of an ester.
7) What is the difference between plant oils and animal fats in terms of bonding?
8) What is the difference between an exothermic and an endothermic reaction? Give an example of each.
9) Sketch an energy level diagram for an exothermic reaction.
10) Explain, in terms of energy, how a catalyst works.
11) What is a reversible reaction?
12) What is a dynamic equilibrium?
13) What is the difference between a strong and a weak acid? Give an example of each.
14) What is the difference between qualitative and quantitative analysis?
15) What is meant by the phrase 'standard procedure'? Why are they important?
16) What are the two phases in chromatography?
17) What are the mobile and stationary phases in paper chromatography and thin-layer chromatography?
18)*What is the R_f value of a chemical that moves 4.5 cm when the solvent moves 12 cm?
19) What are the mobile and stationary phases in gas chromatography?
20) What is meant by 'retention time'?
21) What does the area under a peak on a gas chromatography chromatogram show?
22)*What is the concentration (in g/dm^3) of a solution containing 92 g of HCl in 650 cm^3?
23) Outline how to make a standard solution.
24)a) Briefly describe how you would carry out a titration between 25 cm^3 of 11.2 g/dm^3 KOH and a solution of HCl with an unknown concentration.
   b)* From a titration, you know that it takes 48.9 cm^3 of HCl to neutralise 25 cm^3 of 11.2 g/dm^3 KOH. What is the concentration of HCl used?
25) How would you estimate the degree of uncertainty in a set of results?
26) What is meant by the term 'bulk chemical'? Give two examples of bulk chemicals.
27) What are 'fine chemicals'? Give an example.
28) Describe the stages involved in producing chemicals in industry.
29) Give eight points you should consider when deciding whether a process is sustainable.
30) Why is there a limit to the concentration of ethanol that can be made using fermentation? How can the concentration be increased? Sketch a diagram of the apparatus you could use.
31) Describe how ethanol is made from crude oil. What conditions are needed?
32) Make a table to compare the sustainability of the three methods of ethanol production (fermentation of sugar, fermentation of waste biomass, and from ethane).

* Answers on page 68.

Module P7 — Observing the Universe

Observing the Sky

It's easy to see why people thought we were at the centre of the Universe for ages. The Sun, Moon and stars all seem to orbit around us — but really it's all down to the Earth's spin.

A Sidereal Day is the Time Taken for the Earth to Spin Once

1) If you looked at the night sky for long enough, you'd see distant stars appear to cross the sky. Astronomers have known for years that it's not the stars that move, but the Earth that spins on its axis.

2) For a star to get to the same position in the sky, the Earth needs to spin 360°. The time taken for this to happen is called a sidereal day.

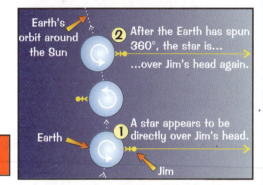

A sidereal day is the time taken for a star to return to the same position in the sky. It's about 23 hours and 56 minutes.

The Sun and Moon Appear to Cross the Sky at Different Speeds

1) It's not just the stars — the Sun and Moon also appear to cross the sky from east to west.

2) The Sun seems to move more slowly across the sky than distant stars — it takes 24 hours to get to the same position in the sky, a whole 4 minutes longer. This is called a solar day.

A solar day is the time taken for the Sun to appear at the same position in the sky. It's 24 hours.

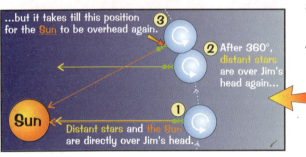

3) Solar and sidereal days are different because the Earth orbits the Sun as well as spinning on its axis.

4) The Earth orbits the Sun in the same direction as it spins — so the Earth needs to spin slightly more than 360° before the Sun appears at the same position in the sky.

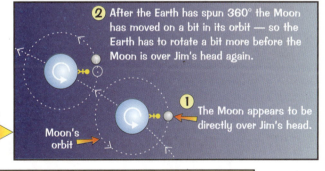

5) The Moon seems to go more slowly than the Sun, taking about 25 hours to appear at the same position in the sky.

6) This is because the Moon orbits the Earth in the same direction as the Earth is rotating.

The Stars You Can See in the Sky Change During the Year

1) As the Earth moves around the Sun, the direction we face changes slightly each day.

2) This means we can see a slightly different patch of sky each night — we see different stars.

3) An Earth year is the time it takes the Earth to orbit the Sun once, so on the same day each year you should be able to see the same stars in the night sky.

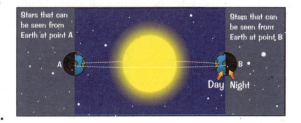

All this spinning is making me dizzy...

The ancient Egyptians thought the Sun was a god called Ra riding a golden chariot across the sky. Don't try putting that in your exam though... you won't get any marks.

Eclipses and the Moon

Some more spinning and orbiting, but this time it's the Moon's turn...

The Phases of the Moon

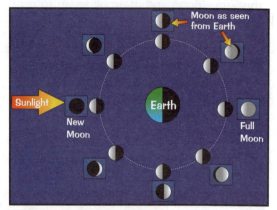

1) The Moon doesn't glow itself — it only reflects light from the Sun. Only the half facing the Sun is lit up, leaving the other half in shadow.
2) As the Moon orbits the Earth, we see different amounts of the Moon's dark and lit-up surfaces.
3) You see a 'full moon' when the whole of the lit-up surface is facing the Earth, and a 'new moon' when the dark half faces us.
4) The rest of the phases are in between these two extremes.

Eclipses Happen When Light from the Sun is Blocked

There are two main types of eclipse: lunar and solar.

LUNAR ECLIPSE

As it orbits, the Moon sometimes passes into the Earth's shadow. The Earth blocks sunlight from the Moon, so almost no light is reflected from the Moon and it just seems to disappear. A total lunar eclipse is where no direct sunlight can reach the Moon. More often, the Moon isn't fully in the Earth's shadow so only part of it appears dark — a partial lunar eclipse.

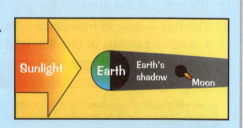

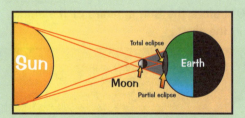

SOLAR ECLIPSE

The Moon is (purely by chance) just the right size and distance away that when it passes between the Sun and the Earth, it can block out the Sun. This is called a solar eclipse. From some parts of the Earth the Sun is completely blocked — a total solar eclipse. From many places on Earth only part of the Sun will be blocked — a partial solar eclipse. From most places on Earth the Sun won't be blocked at all.

Eclipses Don't Happen Very Often

1) It's not every day you see the Sun being blotted out of the sky by the Moon.
2) The Moon orbits the Earth at a slight angle to Earth's orbit around the Sun. So most of the time the Sun, Moon and Earth don't line up to cause a lunar or solar eclipse.
3) Partial eclipses happen a bit more often as they don't have to line up perfectly for this.
4) Even when there is a solar eclipse, there's only a very small region on Earth from which it can be seen. There might be a total solar eclipse in China but we'd hardly notice anything in the UK.

Aaaargh — the Sun's been eaten by a giant sky monster...

If you ever get the chance to see a total solar eclipse, it's amazing (but don't look directly at the Sun). If you want to see it in the UK though, don't buy your popcorn just yet — you'll have to wait 'til 2090...

Module P7 — Observing the Universe

Coordinates in Astronomy

This page is a bit tricky, but stick with it...

The Positions of Stars are Measured by Angles Seen from Earth

1) The positions of stars are measured by angles seen from Earth. It's just like latitude and longitude on Earth — only for the sky.

2) The sky appears to turn as the Earth spins — so astronomers picked two fixed positions to measure from:
   - **THE POLE STAR** is a star that doesn't seem to move because it's almost directly above the North Pole (and the spin axis) of Earth.
   - **THE CELESTIAL EQUATOR** is an imaginary plane running across the sky, extending out from the Earth's equator.

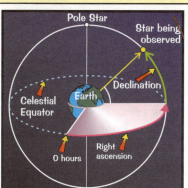

3) The two angles used to measure positions in the sky are:
   - Declination — Celestial latitude, measured in degrees.
   - Right Ascension — Celestial longitude (the 'how much across' angle), measured in degrees or time.

   It might sound a bit weird having an angle as a time, but it's possible because the Earth turns through 360° every 24 hours. Right ascension increases the further east on the sky you go.

Planets Seem to Move in Complicated Patterns

1) All the planets in the Solar System orbit the Sun in the same direction but at different speeds. The closer to the Sun, the quicker the planet.

2) Even without a telescope, you can often see the 'naked eye' planets — Mercury, Venus, Mars, Jupiter and Saturn. To track a planet as it goes across the sky, set your alarm clock and note down its position at the same (sidereal) time each night. (That way you rule out the Earth's spin making it cross the sky.) You'll find that the planets seem to gradually travel from west to east.

3) Every so often, though, a planet seems to change direction and go the other way for a bit, making a loop or squiggle in its track before carrying on as normal. (This only happens with the outer planets — Mars to Neptune.)

4) It happens because both the planet and Earth are moving around the Sun — so we're seeing the motion of the planet relative to Earth.

5) Mars appears to change direction once every two or so years. Slower-moving planets further out 'change direction' less frequently.

① From Earth, Mars appears to move to the left (west to east) compared to distant background stars.

② About three months later, Earth 'overtakes' Mars, and so Mars appears to change direction (travelling from east to west).

③ After another few months, Earth moves 'vertically down' while Mars is still moving 'horizontally', so Mars once again appears to move to the left (west to east).

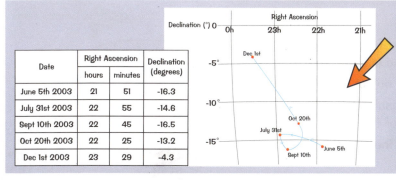

Date	Right Ascension		Declination (degrees)
	hours	minutes	
June 5th 2003	21	51	-16.3
July 31st 2003	22	55	-14.6
Sept 10th 2003	22	45	-16.5
Oct 20th 2003	22	25	-13.2
Dec 1st 2003	23	29	-4.3

The diagram shows the loop Mars made in 2003. You can tell just from the table of data that Mars has changed direction. Mars travels east (right ascension increases) — then changes direction and moves west (right ascension decreases) before moving east again (right ascension increases).

It's all just loops and squiggles...

Time is an angle? Hmm. And the planets are a bit like athletes running at different speeds on a race track and lapping each other — make sure you can explain how this causes those loops and squiggles.

Converging Lenses

Lenses are used in telescopes. No, really... They change the direction of light rays by refraction.

Converging Lenses Bring Light Rays Together

1) A converging lens is convex — it gets fatter towards the middle. It causes rays of light to converge (come together) to a focus.
2) All lenses have a principal axis, a line which passes straight through the middle of the lens.
3) The focal point of a lens is where rays initially parallel to the principal axis meet. (All lenses have two focal points, one in front and one behind the lens.)

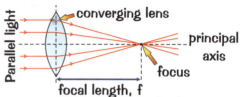

4) The focal length of a lens is just the distance between the middle of the lens and its focal point.
5) Focal length is related to power. The more powerful the lens, the more strongly it converges rays of light, so the shorter the focal length.

 E.g. for a lens with focal length f = 0.2 m, power = 1 ÷ 0.2 = 5 D.
(D stands for dioptres, the unit for lens power.)

$$\text{Power} = \frac{1}{\text{Focal length}}$$

6) To make a more powerful lens from a certain material like glass, you just have to make it with more strongly curved surfaces.

Drawing Ray Diagrams for Light from Objects in Space

A lot of objects like stars are so far away that you can think of them as just dots of light (point sources). Light rays from them are effectively parallel by the time they reach Earth. This makes it nice and easy to draw ray diagrams of the light being focused with a converging lens — here's how:

Point Source

1) Mark the focal point on the principal axis. Draw 3 parallel rays from the star (or whatever it is) — one to the centre of the lens, one towards the top and one towards the bottom. Only draw the rays going as far as the middle of the lens.
2) The middle ray doesn't get refracted, so just extend this ray past the focal point of the lens.
3) Draw in the rest of the top and bottom rays, making them meet the middle ray above or below the focal point. The image is formed at this point — and it's a real image, as all the rays actually meet there.

Extended Source

It's almost exactly the same for light from extended sources (anything that you can't just pretend is a dot, e.g. a galaxy).

1) Treat two opposite edges of the object as point sources.
2) As before, the parallel rays for each edge will meet in line with (or at) the focal point of the lens.
3) A real image is formed between the two points where the rays meet.

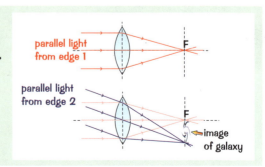

Convex lenses — keepin' it real...

A real image — instead of a fake image? Well, kind of. Sometimes virtual images are formed — where light rays appear to have come from. This is really useful in the refracting telescope (see next page).

Telescopes

Telescopes use <u>convex lenses</u> or <u>curved mirrors</u> to <u>magnify</u> light from space. Here's how.

A <u>Simple Refracting Telescope</u> Uses <u>Two</u> <u>Converging Lenses</u>

1) A simple refracting telescope is made up of two <u>convex</u> lenses — an <u>objective lens</u> and an <u>eye lens</u>.
2) The lenses are <u>aligned</u> to have the same <u>principal axis</u> and are placed so that their focal points are in the <u>same place</u>.
3) Many objects in space are so <u>far away</u> that by the time their light arrives on Earth, the <u>light rays</u> are effectively <u>parallel</u>.
4) The <u>objective lens</u> converges these parallel rays to form a <u>real image</u> between the two lenses.
5) The <u>eye lens</u> is much more <u>powerful</u> than the objective lens. It acts as a <u>magnifying glass</u> on the real image and makes a <u>virtual image</u> — where the light entering the eye lens <u>appears</u> to have come from.
6) The <u>angular magnification</u>, M, of the telescope can be calculated from the <u>focal lengths</u> of the objective lens, f_o, and the eye lens, f_e.

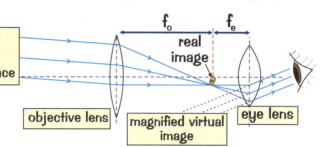

$$\text{Magnification} = \frac{\text{Focal length of objective lens}}{\text{Focal length of eye lens}}$$

EXAMPLE 1: An astronomer uses a refracting telescope to look at a distant star. If $f_o = 4.5$ m and $f_e = 0.1$ m, find the angular magnification of the telescope.

ANSWER: Angular magnification = $f_o \div f_e$ = 4.5 ÷ 0.1 = <u>45</u>

EXAMPLE 2: Geoff makes a telescope which has a 0.2 D objective lens and an 8 D eye lens. What is the magnification of Geoff's telescope?

ANSWER: $P = 1 \div f$, so $f = 1 \div P$. So $f_o = 1 \div 0.2 = $ <u>5 m</u>, $f_e = 1 \div 8 = $ <u>0.125 m</u>.
Angular magnification = $f_o \div f_e$ = 5 ÷ 0.125 = <u>40</u>

See right at the bottom of the page for a shortcut for doing this one.

Most Astronomical Telescopes Use a <u>Concave Mirror</u>

1) Most astronomical telescopes use a <u>concave mirror</u> instead of a convex <u>objective</u> lens.
2) <u>Concave</u> mirrors are shiny on the <u>inside</u> of the curve. Parallel rays of light shining on a <u>concave</u> mirror reflect and <u>converge</u>.
3) Concave mirrors are like a portion of a <u>sphere</u>. The centre of the sphere is the <u>centre of curvature</u>, C.
4) The centre of the mirror's surface is called the <u>vertex</u>.
5) Halfway between the centre of curvature and the vertex is the <u>focal point</u>, F. These points all lie on the <u>axis</u>.
6) Rays <u>parallel</u> to the mirror's axis, e.g. those from a distant star, reflect and <u>meet at the focal point</u> (as with lenses).
7) By putting a <u>lens</u> near the focal point of the mirror to act as an <u>eyepiece</u>, you can form a <u>magnified image</u> — just as in the simple refracting telescope above.

<u>Important stuff this — come on, focus, focus...</u>

There's an alternative <u>magnification formula</u> you can use if you're given the <u>powers</u> rather than focal lengths. It'll save faffing about: Magnification = Power$_{eye}$ ÷ Power$_{objective}$. (It's just upside down.)

Module P7 — Observing the Universe

Astronomical Distances and Brightness

Stars — they're bright and really far away. But are the brighter ones really brighter or just closer...

The Distance to Nearby Stars can be Measured by Parallax

1) As you saw way back in Module P1, parallax is an apparent change in position of an object against a distant background. In astronomy:

> The parallax angle is half the angle moved against distant background stars over 6 months (at the opposite ends of the Earth's orbit). The nearer an object is to you, the greater the angle.

2) This angle is often measured in arcseconds rather than degrees:
$$1 \text{ arcsecond} = 1'' = \left(\frac{1}{3600}\right)^\circ$$

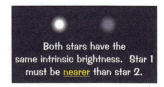

3) Parallax is useful for calculating the distance to nearby stars. The smaller the parallax angle, the more distant the star is. Astronomers often use a unit of distance called a parsec. It's about 3 light years — a really long way in other words. Distances between stars are normally a few parsecs.

> A parsec (pc) is the distance to a star with a parallax angle of 1 arcsecond.

4) You can calculate the distance to a star (in parsecs) using this equation:
$$\text{distance (pc)} = \left(\frac{1}{\text{angle (arcsec)}}\right)$$

EXAMPLE: Mr Moore measures the parallax of a star to be 0.4". How far away is the star in parsecs?

ANSWER: $\text{distance (pc)} = \left(\frac{1}{0.4''}\right) = 2.5 \text{ pc}$

Observed Brightness Depends on the Distance to the Star

1) The intrinsic brightness of a star (how bright it'd seem if you could go right up to it) depends on how big the star is and how hot it is. The bigger and hotter it is, the more energy it gives out, and so the brighter it is.

2) As you move away from a star, it looks dimmer — because the energy reaching you gets less (as it spreads out through space). So the observed brightness of a star seen from Earth depends on its intrinsic brightness and how far away it is.

Both stars have the same intrinsic brightness. Star 1 must be nearer than star 2.

3) So if you looked at two stars with the same intrinsic brightness but one was further away than the other, the more distant star would look dimmer.

A Cepheid Variable Star's Pulse Depends on Its Brightness

1) A group of stars called cepheid variables pulse in brightness — they get brighter and then dimmer over a period of several days.

2) How quickly they pulse is directly linked to their intrinsic brightness. The brighter the star, the longer the time between pulses (the pulse period).

3) So, if you see two cepheid variable stars with the same apparent brightness that pulse at different rates, you know that the star with the longer pulse period must have the higher intrinsic brightness. So the star with the longer pulse period must be further away.

4) Astronomers can work out the distance to a cepheid variable by comparing the intrinsic brightness (worked out from the pulse period) and the observed brightness of the star.

I'm not dim — I'm just really far away...

Cepheid variables are really useful — you can use them to work out the distance to whatever big ball of gas they might be in. These cheeky chaps helped solve one of the most famous debates in astronomy...

Module P7 — Observing the Universe

The Scale of the Universe

We mightn't know exactly how big, but we know the Universe is biiiiiiiiiiiig.

Telescopes Showed That the Sun is a Star in the Milky Way

1) If you went out in the countryside on a clear night you could probably see about 1500 stars (if you've got good eyesight). If you looked with a small telescope, you could probably see over half a million.
2) The more stars you can see, the more you notice that they're not evenly dotted about the sky. Most of the stars appear to be concentrated in a bright strip across the sky — the Milky Way.
3) Away from this strip, the number of visible stars is much smaller.
4) Our Sun is just one of the approximately 10^{11} stars in the galaxy (this was worked out after a lot of peering through telescopes).
5) The Milky Way is actually a spiral galaxy. But because we're part of its disc, we see it edge on as a bright strip in the sky.

The Curtis-Shapley Debate

In the 1920s there was a debate about the size and structure of the Universe, led by two famous American astronomers — Harlow Shapley and Heber Curtis. Through telescopes, people had seen some faint, fuzzy objects that they called nebulae. Some of these objects looked spiral-shaped but some were just blobs. Shapley and Curtis argued about what these nebulae were and where they were:

Shapley's Argument

1) Shapley believed the Universe was just one gigantic galaxy about 100 000 parsecs across.
2) He reckoned our Sun and Solar System were far from the centre of the galaxy.
3) He believed that nebulae were huge clouds of gas and dust. These clouds were relatively nearby and actually part of the Milky Way.

Curtis' Argument

1) Curtis thought the Universe was made up of many galaxies.
2) He thought our galaxy was smaller than Shapley suggested — about 10 000 pc across, with the Sun at or very near the centre.
3) The spiral nebulae were other very distant galaxies, completely separate from the Milky Way.

And the winner is..... well both of them really:

1) Shapley was right that the Solar System is far from the centre of our galaxy, but Curtis was right that there are many galaxies in the Universe (at least 100 000 000 000 of them).
2) Curtis was also right about spiral nebulae — Hubble showed that they're really far away (see next page). (The debate wasn't properly over until the 1930s, though, when better telescopes meant we could see the nebulae clearly, rather than just as blurry blobs.)

The Milky Way — not just a tasty snack...

At least it was all sorted in the end, and now it's a joy for you to learn instead... well, maybe not.

The Scale of the Universe

Edwin Hubble was possibly the most famous astronomer ever (apart from our Patrick with his xylophone).

Hubble Showed There Were Objects Outside the Galaxy

1) Hubble helped solve the Curtis-Shapley debate with his observations of the Andromeda nebula.
2) Using images taken using the largest telescope at the time, he found that this spiral-shaped fuzzy blob contained many stars, some of which were Cepheid variables (see page 50).
3) Hubble calculated the distance to the Andromeda nebula by working out the distance to the Cepheid variables within it, using the relationship between their brightness and pulse frequency (see page 50).
4) He found it was about 2.5 million light years away — much further than any stars in our galaxy.
5) He studied other spiral nebulae and found a similar result — they were all too far away to be part of the Milky Way, and so must be separate spiral galaxies themselves.

Distant Galaxies are Moving Away from Us

1) When a galaxy is moving away from us the wavelength of the light from it changes — the light becomes redder. This is called red shift.
2) By seeing how much the light has been red-shifted, you can work out the recession velocity of the galaxy (how quickly it's moving away). The greater the red shift, the greater the speed of recession.
3) Using red shift, Hubble compared the speed and the distances for many distant galaxies and found a pattern:

> The more distant the galaxy, the faster it moves away from us.

4) Red shift is fairly easy to measure, so a galaxy's recession velocity can be calculated easily enough. The distance to a distant galaxy can be found from its recession velocity using Hubble's law:

> Speed of recession (km/s) = Hubble constant (s^{-1}) × distance (km)

The value of the Hubble constant is roughly 2×10^{-18} s^{-1}.

EXAMPLE 1: A galaxy is 1.5×10^{20} km away.
Use the Hubble constant to estimate the galaxy's speed of recession.
ANSWER: Speed of recession = $2 \times 10^{-18} \times 1.5 \times 10^{20}$ = **300 km/s**.

EXAMPLE 2: Find the distance to a galaxy which has a recession velocity of **475 km/s**.
ANSWER: Rearrange the equation: Distance = Speed of recession / Hubble constant
= $475 \div (2 \times 10^{-18})$ = **2.375×10^{20} km**.

5) The value of the Hubble constant is still being researched. There are many different ways to calculate it, e.g. using Cepheid variable data from distant galaxies. Unfortunately the different methods all come up with slightly different answers.
6) The distances to stuff in space are enormous. They're so big that astronomers tend to use units of megaparsecs when talking about distances to objects outside the Milky Way. 1 megaparsec (Mpc) is about 3×10^{19} km. The distance to the nearest spiral galaxy is just under 0.8 Mpc.

Hubble bubble toil and trouble...

Hubble was well clever — he sorted out the Curtis–Shapley squabble, made up a really useful law, and even made Einstein feel like a bit of a fool. So don't worry if this all seems a bit confusing — just keep having a bash and soon you'll be master of the Universe. Well, master of Hubble's law anyway.

Gas Behaviour

Particles in gases, absolute zero and the Kelvin scale of temperature — ooh, sounds like fun...

Absolute Zero is as Cold as Stuff Can Get — 0 Kelvin

1) If you increase the temperature of something, you give its particles more kinetic energy — they move about more quickly or vibrate more. In the same way, if you cool a substance down, you're reducing the kinetic energy of the particles.
2) The coldest that anything can ever get is −273 °C — this temperature is known as absolute zero. At absolute zero, atoms have as little kinetic energy as it's possible to get.
3) Absolute zero is the start of the Kelvin scale of temperature.
4) A temperature change of 1 °C is also a change of 1 kelvin. The two scales are pretty similar — the only difference is where the zero is.
5) To convert from degrees Celsius to kelvins, just add 273. And to convert from kelvins to degrees Celsius, just subtract 273.

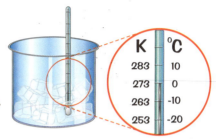

	Absolute zero	Freezing point of water	Boiling point of water
Celsius scale	−273 °C	0 °C	100 °C
Kelvin scale	0 K	273 K	373 K

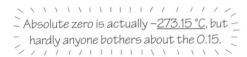
Absolute zero is actually −273.15 °C, but hardly anyone bothers about the 0.15.

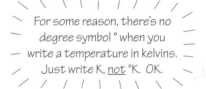
For some reason, there's no degree symbol ° when you write a temperature in kelvins. Just write K, not °K. OK.

A Decrease in Volume Gives an Increase in Pressure

1) As gas particles move about, they bang into each other and whatever else happens to get in the way.
2) Gas particles are very light, but they sure ain't massless. When they collide with something, they exert a force on it. In a sealed container, gas particles smash against the container's walls — creating an outward pressure.
3) And if you put the same amount of gas in a bigger container, the pressure will decrease, cos there'll be fewer collisions between the gas particles and the container's walls. When the volume's reduced, the particles get more squashed up and so they hit the walls more often, hence the pressure increases.

Increasing the Temperature Increases the Pressure

1) The pressure of a gas depends on how fast the particles are going and how often they hit the walls of the container they're in.
2) If you heat a gas, the particles move faster and have more kinetic energy. This increase in kinetic energy means the particles hit the container walls harder and more often, creating more pressure.
3) In fact, temperature (in kelvins) and pressure are proportional — double the temperature (in K), and you double the pressure too.

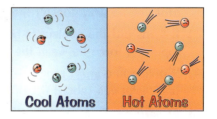

Absolute zero — nought, zilch, not a sausage...

It's weird to think that things don't get any colder than zero kelvins (or −273 °C). I mean, what if you had a really top-of-the-range fridge that went really cold... You could set it to −273 °C, put in, say, a jelly, and then turn the fridge down a bit more. What would happen to the jelly... it's all weird...

Module P7 — Observing the Universe

Structure of the Atom

Atoms, alpha particles, the strong force and some plum pudding — mmm, tasty...

Rutherford Scattering and the Demise of the Plum Pudding

1) In 1804, John Dalton suggested that matter was made up of tiny spheres ("atoms") that couldn't be broken up. Nearly 100 years later, J J Thomson discovered that electrons could be removed from atoms. So Dalton's theory wasn't quite right (atoms could be broken up). Thomson suggested that atoms were spheres of positive charge with tiny negative electrons stuck in them like plums in a plum pudding.

2) That "plum pudding" theory didn't last very long though. In 1909 Ernest Rutherford and his merry men Geiger and Marsden tried firing alpha particles — which are positive — at thin gold foil. Most of the alpha particles just went straight through, but the odd one came straight back at them, which was frankly a bit of a shocker for Ernie and his pals.

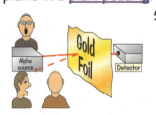

3) Being a pretty clued-up guy, Rutherford realised this meant:

- Most of the mass of a gold atom was concentrated at the centre in a tiny nucleus. The rest of the atom must be mainly empty space — as most of the alpha particles went straight through the foil.
- The nucleus had to have a positive charge — otherwise the positively charged alpha particles wouldn't be repelled by the nucleus and wouldn't scatter.

The Nuclear Model of the Atom

Yep, this was in P3 — but you need to remember it here too.

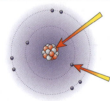

The nucleus is tiny but it makes up most of the mass of the atom. It contains protons (which are positively charged) and neutrons (which are neutral) — which gives it an overall positive charge.

The rest of the atom is mostly empty space. The negative electrons whizz round the outside of the nucleus really fast. They give the atom its overall size.

The Nucleus is Held Together by the Strong Force

1) The electrons are kept in orbit around the nucleus by the attractive electrical force between the positive nucleus and the negative electrons (opposite charges attract). If the electrons are given enough energy, they can overcome this attractive force and be removed from the atom — this is called ionisation (see your Module P2 notes).

2) But what about the nucleus I hear you cry... it contains positively charged particles, which repel each other — so why doesn't the nucleus just split apart with protons whooshing off in all directions?

3) It turns out the nucleus is held together by an attractive force much greater than the electrical repulsion force between the protons. This force is called the strong force.

4) It only has a short range — it can only hold protons and neutrons together when they're separated by tiny distances (about 0.000000000000001 m). At larger separations, the strong force disappears.

5) At very small separations, the strong interaction must be repulsive — otherwise there would be nothing to stop it crushing the nucleus to a point.

Alpha Scattering — a bit like a game of miniature bowls...

So — atoms make up everything, they have a tiny positive nucleus and electrons whizzing around it. Easy... but the thing that freaks me out is that atoms are mostly empty space, so really everything from air, to traffic cones, to me and you, is mainly a load of empty space. Weird...

Module P7 — Observing the Universe

Fusion and Stellar Structure

What could you want on one page? Einstein, stars, fusion and a railway bridge in Scotland....

Scientists Only 'Discovered' Fusion in the Early 20th Century

1) Scientists used to believe that the Sun just burned its own material. Then in the 19th century, they realised that the Sun would have needed an impossible amount of fuel to have kept burning for so long.
2) In the early 20th century, Einstein realised that mass could be converted to energy.
3) Lots of other clever people put the rest of the puzzle together. It was suggested that hydrogen is turned into helium inside the Sun, and that when this happens some mass gets 'lost' (they knew this by comparing the masses of hydrogen and helium atoms). Perhaps the missing mass was being changed into energy — and powering the Sun...
4) Hans Bethe did some hard sums to explain how fusion (see below) must be the power source of the Sun — and got a Nobel prize for his trouble.

Nuclei Have to be Brought Close Together to Fuse

1) Two nuclei can combine to create a larger nucleus — this is called nuclear fusion. In the core of the Sun, hydrogen nuclei fuse into helium nuclei and release energy.
2) It's not just hydrogen atoms that fuse — stars fuse other elements when the hydrogen runs out (see page 57).
3) All nuclei are positively charged — they only contain neutrons and protons. Like charges repel, so there is a repulsive electrical force between two nuclei, trying to stop them being brought together.
4) Nuclei can only fuse if they overcome this electrical force and get close enough for the attractive strong force (see page 54) to hold them together. For that you need lots of energy — a high temperature.

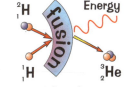

nuclei repel each other.

Nuclei brought close enough for the strong force to hold them together.

A Star Has Different Zones

A star is made up of a core surrounded by different layers:

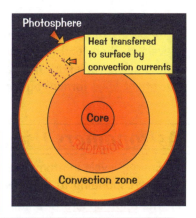

1) **THE CORE** — Most of the fusion in a star takes place in the core. The pressure from the weight of the rest of the star makes the core hot and dense. This means that the nuclei in the core are close enough (and have enough energy) to fuse together.

2) **THE CONVECTION ZONE** — Energy released from fusion in the core is transferred by convection and radiation. Energy is transferred to the surface of the star by convection currents in the convection zone. The convection zone is a bit cooler than the core.

3) **PHOTOSPHERE** — the outer region, or 'surface' of a star, from where energy is radiated into space. This is the part of the Sun that we see from Earth. The photosphere is constantly churning like the surface of boiling water — mostly because of the constant rising and falling of material in the convection zone below. The photosphere is cooler than the convection zone.

The Forth Bridge — now that's a stellar structure...

If stars don't get hot enough, fusion doesn't take place and they won't become stars. Stars also actually have a radiation zone between the core and convection zone — but you don't need to worry about it.

Star Spectra

The light from stars doesn't just make the sky look pretty, it can actually tell you what stars are made of...

Continuous Spectra Contain All Possible Frequencies

1) All hot objects like stars emit radiation. Hot objects emit a continuous range of frequencies — a continuous spectrum (it doesn't have any gaps).
2) Hot objects always emit more of one frequency than any other. This wavelength is called the peak frequency.
3) The peak frequency emitted by an object depends on its temperature. The higher the temperature, the more energy the photons radiated will have, and so the higher the peak frequency.
4) The intensity (see Module P2) or brightness also depends on temperature — hotter things glow more.
5) For example, we can tell how hot a star is by looking at its colour:
   red = has a low frequency = a cool star (well... still hot enough to cook you and your toast)
   blue = has a high frequency = scorchio (that's hot). The Sun's a fairly cool star — it looks yellowy.

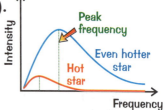

Line Spectra — Electrons Moving Between Energy Levels

1) An atom contains electrons which move around a tiny positive nucleus.
2) Electrons can only be in certain energy levels (or shells) around the nucleus — with the lowest energy levels nearest the nucleus.

ABSORPTION SPECTRA — At high temperatures, electrons become excited and jump into higher energy levels by absorbing radiation. Because there are only certain energy levels an electron can occupy, electrons absorb a particular frequency of radiation to get to a higher energy level.

You can 'see' this if a continuous spectrum of visible light shines through a gas — the electrons in the gas atoms absorb certain frequencies of the light, making gaps in the otherwise continuous spectrum. These gaps appear as dark lines.

Absorption line

EMISSION SPECTRA — Electrons are unstable in the higher energy levels so they tend to fall from higher to lower levels, losing energy by emitting radiation of a particular frequency. This gives a series of bright lines formed by the emitted frequencies.

An emission spectrum

Astronomers Use Spectra to Work Out What Stars are Made Of

1) Energy levels in atoms are different for each element — so each element has its own line spectrum (corresponding to the energies needed for electrons to get from one energy level to another).
2) The photosphere of a star emits a continuous spectrum of radiation. This radiation passes through the gases in a star's atmosphere, which produces emission and absorption lines in the spectrum.
3) By looking at the position of these lines in the star's spectrum, you can work out what elements are present in the star's atmosphere — by comparing it with known spectra in the lab.

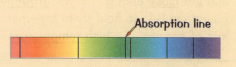
Stellar spectrum (containing H, He and Na)

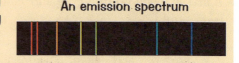
Hydrogen
Helium
Sodium

What do you call a star detective? In-Spectra...

It's really useful stuff this line spectra business — it's as near as you can get to flying to a star, getting out your bucket and spade and having a good dig around to see what it's made of.

Module P7 — Observing the Universe

The Birth and Death of Stars

Stars — they're born, get middle aged (without feeling the need to buy a sports car) and then go bang.

Stars Begin as Clouds of Dust and Gas

1) Stars are born in a cloud of dust and gas (most of which was left when previous stars blew themselves apart in supernovae — see below). The denser regions of the cloud contract very slowly into clumps under the force of gravity.
2) When these clumps get dense enough, the cloud breaks up into protostars that continue to contract and heat up as the pressure increases (see page 53).
3) Eventually the temperature at the centre of a protostar reaches a few million degrees, and hydrogen nuclei start to fuse together to form helium (see page 55).
4) This releases an enormous amount of energy and creates enough outward pressure (radiation pressure) to stop the gravitational collapse.
5) The star has now reached the MAIN SEQUENCE stage. It stays like that, relatively unchanging, while it fuses hydrogen into helium.

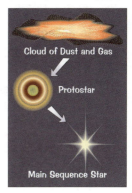

Stars Fuse Other Elements When the Hydrogen Runs Out

OK, you've seen this before way back in Module P1, but now you need to know it in a bit more detail...

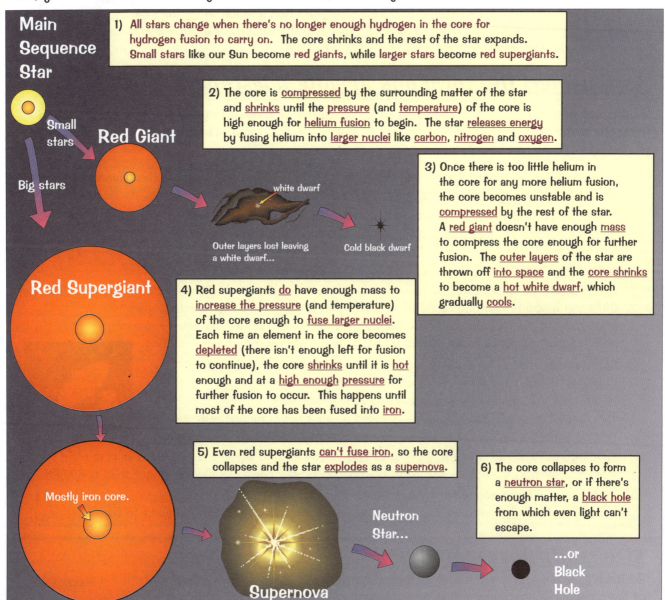

1) All stars change when there's no longer enough hydrogen in the core for hydrogen fusion to carry on. The core shrinks and the rest of the star expands. Small stars like our Sun become red giants, while larger stars become red supergiants.
2) The core is compressed by the surrounding matter of the star and shrinks until the pressure (and temperature) of the core is high enough for helium fusion to begin. The star releases energy by fusing helium into larger nuclei like carbon, nitrogen and oxygen.
3) Once there is too little helium in the core for any more helium fusion, the core becomes unstable and is compressed by the rest of the star. A red giant doesn't have enough mass to compress the core enough for further fusion. The outer layers of the star are thrown off into space and the core shrinks to become a hot white dwarf, which gradually cools.
4) Red supergiants do have enough mass to increase the pressure (and temperature) of the core enough to fuse larger nuclei. Each time an element in the core becomes depleted (there isn't enough left for fusion to continue), the core shrinks until it is hot enough and at a high enough pressure for further fusion to occur. This happens until most of the core has been fused into iron.
5) Even red supergiants can't fuse iron, so the core collapses and the star explodes as a supernova.
6) The core collapses to form a neutron star, or if there's enough matter, a black hole from which even light can't escape.

Module P7 — Observing the Universe

Observing with Telescopes

Sometimes, no matter how hard you squint, your eyes just aren't good enough — you need a telescope.

To Detect Faint Sources You Need a Wide Aperture

1) Some objects in the sky are so distant and faint, only a tiny amount of radiation from them reaches us.
2) To collect enough of the radiation from these objects to see them, you need to use a telescope with a huge objective lens (or mirror). The diameter of the objective lens is called the aperture. The bigger the aperture, the more radiation can get into the telescope and the better the image formed.
3) Making large lenses is difficult and expensive, whereas big mirrors are much easier to make accurately. This is one of the reasons why many telescopes have a concave mirror instead of a lens (see page 49).

Aperture Size Must be Much Larger Than Wavelength

1) Whenever radiation passes through a gap, it diffracts (see your Module P6 notes). Radiation entering a telescope is diffracted at the edges of the aperture — causing the image to blur.
2) If you looked at radiation from a point source like a star when there was no diffraction, you'd see a bright dot. If you used too small an aperture to look at the star, the dot would be dimmer and surrounded by rings which get dimmer the further away from the image they are.

3) The only way round this problem is to have an aperture that's much wider than the wavelength of radiation you want to look at. This way the radiation passes through the aperture and into your telescope with very little diffraction.

Astronomers Use Local and Remote Telescopes

If you want to use a single local telescope (one nearby that you can easily get to), you can go to the telescope and point it at the object you want to look at. Easy. Most telescopes are now computer controlled — which has lots of advantages:

1) Instead of an astronomer having to always be there, they now just program the telescope to track an object in the sky, then go home for tea (or to bed).
2) Computer control is also very useful when astronomers are using a telescope to do a survey — scanning across large areas of the sky in search of particular objects. For this, the telescope needs to be constantly repositioned to look at different areas of sky. Thanks to computer control, this can just be programmed in too.
3) Astronomers like putting telescopes in remote locations, like on a hilltop in the middle of a desert. Before computers, astronomers had to travel a long way to use these telescopes. Many telescopes can now be operated remotely via the internet. So astronomers can work from the comfort of their own offices, and don't have to spend time or money travelling.
4) Astronomers may need to have many telescopes pointing in the same direction at the same time. This happens a lot in radio astronomy, which uses information from many dishes spread across large distances. This can all be controlled ... you've guessed it, by a beautiful computer.
5) Optical astronomers can only observe during the night. Because the Earth's spinning, astronomers need a network of telescopes around the world — so it's always night for at least one telescope — if they want to observe an object continuously for longer than one night.
6) And finally, without computer control we wouldn't be able to have space telescopes — you can't exactly just wander up there and nudge the telescope left a bit when you want to (see next page).

Size really does matter...

So the bigger the aperture the better. Remember it needs to be large in comparison to the wavelength of the radiation you're looking at — which is why radio telescopes are huuuuuuge.

Module P7 — Observing the Universe

Space Telescopes

The atmosphere might be good for us (blocking out X-rays for instance), but it's a pain for astronomers...

The Atmosphere Can Mess Up Measurements

1) Astronomers need accurate measurements to be able to understand what's going on in space, but our atmosphere can muck up the results.
2) Our atmosphere only lets certain wavelengths of electromagnetic radiation through and blocks all the others. The graph shows how the transparency of the atmosphere varies with wavelength.
3) Some radiation, like radio waves, passes through the atmosphere without much trouble, but visible light can be badly affected.
4) Light gets refracted by water in the atmosphere, which blurs the images. It can also be absorbed by dust particles in the air. Boo hiss.
5) Sites for astronomical observatories on Earth are picked very carefully to try and minimise all these problems (see next page). Another solution is to take measurements from above the atmosphere...

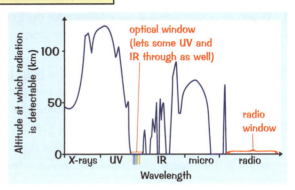

Space Telescopes Have a Clearer View Than Those on Earth

1) If you're trying to look at EM radiation that's blocked or affected by the atmosphere, the thing to do is put your telescope in space, away from the mist and murk down here. The first space telescope (called Hubble) was launched by NASA in 1990. It can see objects that are about a billion times fainter than you can see just by standing in your back garden and looking up on Earth.
2) Hubble is an optical telescope and has a mirror. But because it gets a clear view into space, the mirror can be a lot smaller (and easier to make) than you'd need for a similar telescope on Earth.
3) It's not all plain sailing though. Getting a telescope safely into space is hard. And when things go wrong, it's difficult to get the repair men out. Hubble's first pictures were all fuzzy, because the mirror was the wrong shape. NASA had to send some astronauts up there to fix it. D'oh.
4) Most astronomy is still done using Earth-based telescopes as they're a lot cheaper and easier to build and maintain. Astronomers have also developed good techniques to remove the effects of the atmosphere from their measurements.
5) It's also a lot easier to get a time slot to do your observing on Earth-based telescopes — there are lots more of them so there's much less demand for each one.

There are Many Uncertainties in Space Programmes

1) Space programmes are projects to send things like people, probes and telescopes into space. They're really expensive — the Apollo programme that ended with people walking on the Moon cost about $135 billion in today's money.
2) Governments have to balance paying these sums with other costly priorities like defence, healthcare and coping with natural disasters (which are unpredictable). The funding for space programmes is never guaranteed — there can be cut-backs at any time.
3) Many countries' space programmes are linked (see next page), so cut-backs in one country can have a knock-on effect on the others.

Telescope broken — we can't get the van up there, mate...

Space telescopes are so expensive because you've got to make a telescope that will be strong enough to withstand being blasted into space, but that's lightweight enough too. It's hard work being a boffin.

Observatories and Cooperation

It's just like primary school — astronomers have to learn to play together and share their toys.

Astronomers Need to Work Together

1) Whether it's building a new telescope on Earth or sending people into space, many science projects are too expensive for one country to do alone. These 'big science' projects are only possible if several countries cooperate.
2) By working together, you can get the best people and the best facilities for the job. E.g. scientists in the USA have expertise in launching components and equipment and so would probably be best to advise on getting a probe or object launched into space.
3) The International Space Station is a project led by the US but with the help of 15 other countries, including those in the European Space Agency. Each country is providing different parts of the Station and it's the largest and most expensive international science project in history.

Observatory Locations are Chosen for Astronomical Reasons...

So, you want to build a new observatory on Earth. Where do you put it to be sure of a good view?

1) Optical (visible light) observatories are often put in remote locations, e.g. Roque de los Muchachos in the Canary Islands. The idea is to avoid man-made light pollution (e.g. from street lamps) as well as dust and other particles (e.g. from car exhausts) affecting the observations.
2) Astronomers want as little atmosphere between the observatory and telescope as possible to minimise the distorting and blurring effects it has. So observatories are often built at high altitude (i.e. up mountains) where the atmosphere is thinner and so affects the light less.
E.g. the Mauna Kea site in Hawaii is about 4200 m above sea level.
3) Water in the atmosphere can cause problems by refracting light — so a dry, low-humidity location is good for a telescope. E.g. there are observatories in the Atacama desert in Chile.

...But Other Factors Need to be Taken into Account

Scientists have to live in the real world. They can't just go building observatories in the most remote and awkward places, just because there's a nice view. There are other things to take into account...

1) COST — Observatories aren't cheap to build. Never mind carting all the stuff up a mountain in the middle of nowhere. There's the cost of building, running and eventually closing the observatory.

2) ACCESS — The site will have to have roads built to it (so you can get equipment and people there to build the telescopes) as well as electricity and other facilities. Some places are just too hard to get to.

3) ENVIRONMENT — Scientists have to be careful that building works, etc. will damage the surrounding environment as little as possible, e.g. by disturbance to wildlife or agriculture.

4) SOCIAL — Even with remotely controlled telescopes, there are always going to be a few people who need to work at the telescope site. They'll need facilities such as water, electricity, accommodation, shops, etc., which will be quite expensive to provide. In some areas observatories have benefited the local community — by providing jobs in building and maintaining the observatory.

Hawaii? — Sounds like a sneaky holiday to me...

I might become an astronomer — you get to drink lots of tea, stare into space a lot and go off to exotic holiday destinations to 'observe' stuff... sounds fun.

Module P7 — Observing the Universe

Revision Summary for Module P7

There's a lot of tricky stuff to learn in this section, but at least there are lots of pretty pictures to help. Have a go at these questions, and if you get stuck have a sneaky peek back at the section. Just keep going through them till you can do them all.

1) What is a sidereal day? Why is it shorter than a solar day?
2) Explain why we see different stars at different times of the year.
3) Why does the Moon go through different phases?
4) Describe what causes: a) a solar eclipse b) a lunar eclipse. Why don't eclipses happen very often?
5) What is: a) declination? b) right ascension?
6) Draw and label a diagram to explain why planets occasionally appear to go 'backwards' in the sky.
7)* What is meant by the focal point of a lens? Calculate the power of a lens with a focal length of 0.4 m.
8) Draw a ray diagram for light from a distant extended source being focused by a convex lens. What type of image is formed?
9) Lenses A and B are made of the same glass. Which lens is more powerful? How do you know?
10) Draw a ray diagram to show parallel light rays being magnified by a simple refracting telescope.
11)* A telescope has a 6.25 D eye lens and a 0.4 D objective lens. Calculate its angular magnification.
12) Draw a diagram to show parallel light rays being focused by a concave mirror. Label the centre of curvature, the vertex, the focal point and the axis.
13)* What is parallax? If the parallax angle of a star is 0.5'', how far away is the star in parsecs?
14) What is intrinsic brightness? Write down two factors that influence the apparent brightness of a star.
15) Explain how cepheid variables can be used to work out distances in astronomy.
16) Describe the main differences between the two sides of the Curtis-Shapley debate. How did Hubble help end this debate?
17)* A distant galaxy is 2.4×10^{20} km away. Find the speed of recession of the galaxy, using Hubble constant = 2×10^{-18} s^{-1}.
18) Give two rules about particles in gases, according to kinetic theory.
19) What's absolute zero in °C? What does absolute zero mean in terms of kinetic energy of particles?
20)* Convert the following temperatures into kelvins: a) −89 °C   b) 120 °C   c) 5 °C
21) What two ways are there to increase the pressure of a gas in a sealed container?
22) Describe the Rutherford-Geiger-Marsden alpha scattering experiment and its results.
23) What is the strong force? Why do nuclei need to be brought very close together in order to fuse?
24) What happens in the convection zone of a star? Which part of a star is the hottest?
25) What is the 'peak frequency' of a star?
26) Explain how absorption line spectra can show what elements are present in a star's atmosphere.
27) Describe how a star is formed.
28) A star much larger than the Sun stops fusing hydrogen. Describe the phases the star will go through before becoming a neutron star or a black hole.
29) Give two reasons why astronomers need to use telescopes with a wide aperture.
30) Give two advantages of computer-controlled telescopes.
31) Explain why astronomers can only detect certain wavelengths of radiation from space on Earth.
32) Give one advantage of using space telescopes. Give two reasons why most astronomy is done with Earth-based telescopes.
33) Why do astronomers need to work together on 'big science projects'?
34) Write down two astronomical and two non-astronomical factors that have to be taken into account when choosing a site for an observatory.

* Answers on page 68

Exam Skills

Extract Questions

There might be a question in the exam where you have to answer questions about a chunk of text. If there is, here's what to do....

Questions with Extracts can be Tricky

1) Nowadays, the examiners want you to be able to apply your scientific knowledge, not just recite a load of facts you've learnt. Sneaky.
2) But don't panic — you won't be expected to know stuff you've not been taught.
3) The chunk of text will contain extra info — about real-life applications of science, or details that you haven't been taught. That stuff is there for a reason — for you to use when you're answering the questions.

Here's an idea of what to expect come exam time. Read the article and have a go at the questions.*

Underlining or making notes of the main bits as you read is a good idea.

The MRL for phosmet is 10 000 micrograms per kg.

The same test was repeated several times.

For the first few parts of this question you need to apply what you know about repeating experiments to get reliable results.

The permitted level for phosmet is given in the article — it doesn't matter if you've never heard of phosmet before.

You might not have heard of phosmet, but you should know why pesticides in general are used, and organic alternatives.

Using pesticides helps farmers produce an abundance of high quality crops. There are concerns however that pesticide residues may remain on fruits and vegetables.

There are strict rules about how and when pesticides can be used, and any pesticide residues left on food must be below certain permitted levels known as MRLs (maximum residue levels).

Phosmet is an organophosphate pesticide which is banned in the UK. However, residues of phosmet are found on imported produce and have a MRL of 10 000 micrograms per kilogram.

An imported pear was tested for residues of phosmet. The test was repeated a number of times. Here are the results:

| Residue (micrograms per kg) | 52 | 61 | 53 | 4.3 | 60 |

1 The test was done five times.
   a) Explain why the test was not just done once.
   b) Do you think **all** of the test results are likely to be accurate? Explain your answer.
   c) Find the average of the reliable results.
   d) Is the amount of phosmet below the permitted level?

2 a) Explain how using phosmet can increase crop yields.
   b) Suggest one thing that an organic farmer might do instead of using pesticides such as phosmet.

3 Suggest why using phosmet is banned in the UK.

You know that pesticides can get into the food chain and kill other wildlife, as well as possibly harming humans. This is likely to be why phosmet is banned.

Thinking in an exam — it's not like the old days...

*Answers on page 68.

It's scary when they expect you to think in the exam. But questions like this often have some of the answers hidden in the text, which is always a bonus. Just make sure you read carefully and take your time.

Mathematical Skills

Calculation questions are bound to crop up — especially in the physicsy bits of your exams.
So you need to be able to handle formulas, units and standard form...

Formula Triangles Make Rearranging Equations a Doddle

You'll be given some formulas, but not as triangles — so it makes sense to learn how to put formulas into triangles for yourself. There are two easy rules:

1) If the formula is "A = B×C" then A goes on the top and B×C goes on the bottom.
2) If the formula is "A = B/C" then B must go on the top (because that's the only way it'll give "B divided by something") — and so pretty obviously A and C must go on the bottom.

So... V=I×R turns into: [V / I×R]   W=F×d turns into: [W / F×d]   V=E/Q turns into: [E / V×Q]

HOW TO USE THEM: Cover up the thing you want to find and write down what's left showing.
Example: To find Q from the last one, cover up Q and you get E/V left showing, so "Q = E/V".

Standard Form is Great for Very Big and Very Small Numbers

Standard form is a convenient way of writing very big and very small numbers, e.g.
56 000 000 would be written as 5.6×10^7.
0.000 000 56 would be written as 5.6×10^{-7}.

You need to be able to read and write any number in standard form for your exam.

A number in standard form is always written as: $A \times 10^n$

A is a number between 1 and 10 (though not 10 itself).

n is the number of places the decimal point moves. n is positive if the number is big, and negative if the number is small.

EXAMPLE: Write "35 000 N" in standard form.

Write the number out with its decimal point (in this case 35 000.0).
Move the decimal point until you get a number between 1 and 10 (in this case, 3.5).
The decimal point moves 4 places, so n = 4. 35 000 is a big number, so n is positive.
So 35 000 N = 3.5×10^4 N (the units stay the same).

Unit Prefixes are Often Used Instead of Standard Form

In science, numbers will often have units attached.
So, instead of using standard form, you can add a prefix to your unit.
The prefixes you need to know are:

Prefix	milli-	centi-	kilo-	mega-
Symbol	m	c	k	M
Meaning	one thousandth ($\times 10^{-3}$)	one hundredth ($\times 10^{-2}$)	one thousand ($\times 10^3$)	one million ($\times 10^6$)

So, 23 000 Hz could be written as 23 kHz (just divide the number by 1000).
0.0054 s could be written as 5.4 ms (multiply by 1000).
48 500 000 J could be written as 48.5 MJ (divide by 1 000 000).

Exam Skills

Drawing and Interpreting Graphs

You'll probably get at least one question in the exam where you have to draw or interpret a graph, e.g. read off some values. This kind of thing can be easy marks, but only if you pay attention to the details.

Look at the Axes and Scales When You're Reading Graphs...

When you're confronted with a graph and you have to answer questions about it, make sure you do all these things:

1) This might seem obvious, but read the question and be sure you know what the graph's about.
2) Jot down or highlight what you're finding out.
3) Read the labels on the axes, including any units. The units can be really important if you have to do calculations.
4) Look at the scales — does each little square stand for 10 units, 0.5 units or what? And don't assume that both axes will have the same scale — they probably won't.
5) Now do the questions... and make sure you show your working. For instance, if you drew lines on the graph to work something out, leave them in.

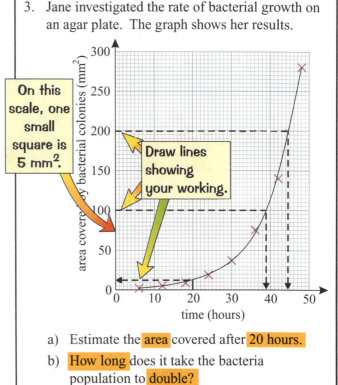

3. Jane investigated the rate of bacterial growth on an agar plate. The graph shows her results.

On this scale, one small square is 5 mm^2.

Draw lines showing your working.

a) Estimate the area covered after 20 hours.
b) How long does it take the bacteria population to double?

...And Choose Them Sensibly When You Draw Graphs

You might be given some data and asked to draw a graph. Don't rush — read the instructions carefully.

1) You might have to pick your own axes and scales. Remember these pointers:

- Always put the thing that's being investigated on the vertical axis (see the example above).
- Label both axes and give the right units.
- Make your graph as big as possible...
- But don't choose a weird scale like 3 units per square — it'll be a nightmare to plot points.

2) Now you can plot the points as crosses, using a sharp pencil.
3) Think whether any of your points look dodgy. If so, have you made a mistake plotting them — check. Or might they have been caused by experimental error...?
4) ...in which case you can ignore them when you're drawing a line of best fit or a smooth curve. (Don't rub dodgy points out — just ignore them when you're thinking where to put the line or curve).

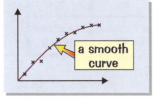

a smooth curve

5) Remember, for graphs in science you don't have to go through all the points. But you do have to use a pencil. And unless you're a fan of throwing away marks for no good reason at all, use a ruler for straight lines.

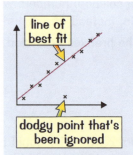

line of best fit

dodgy point that's been ignored

Exam Skills

Exam Skills — Paper Three

Paper Three is known as 'Ideas In Context'. It's a bit odd — but no odder than, say, beetroot.

You'll be Given Some Material in Advance

Before the exam you'll be given a booklet containing some articles that you'll be examined on. Don't just stuff it in the bottom of your bag with your PE kit — start working on it straight away.

The articles could be on any science topic that's related to the material on the specification. They could well be about something that's been in the news recently, or you could get an article about how scientific understanding has developed over time.

So, don't be surprised if some of them seem a bit wacky — they will be related to the stuff you've learned — it might just take you a while to figure out how...

Start work as soon as you get the booklet

1) Read all the articles carefully and slowly — take your time and make sure you understand everything.
2) Look up any words that you don't know.
3) If there are any graphs, tables or figures in the articles then study them carefully. Identify any trends and make sure you know what they show.
4) You don't need to do any extra research on the topics but if you're struggling with the material then a bit of extra reading might help you to understand it — try textbooks and internet searches. Don't get too carried away though — you shouldn't need any extra knowledge to answer the questions.
5) Although you don't need to do research you do need to make sure you've revised the topics that the articles are about. So if there's one about running marathons in hot climates, make sure you've revised homeostasis really thoroughly, in all its glorious detail.
6) Remember to do all of the above for all of the articles — you'll have to answer questions on all of them in the exam.
7) It's a good idea to highlight important things in the booklet and make some notes as you go along, but remember that you can't take the booklet into the exam.

There'll be a mixture of questions in the exam

When you get to the exam you'll be given another copy of the articles, and some questions to go with them.

1) For some of the questions you'll need to extract information from the articles (see page 62).
2) Other questions will be about analysing data or information in the articles (see page 64).
3) Other questions will ask you about related topics from the specification — but you won't be expected to know anything that isn't on the specification or in the article.

I'd prefer an exam where you get the questions in advance...

Paper 3 should hold no fears, providing you've used the time before the exam to swot up on the topics that are covered in the articles. If you're the type who watches the news and stuff then chances are you'll be familiar with some of the issues before you even get the booklet. Even so, get swotting...

Exam Skills

Index

A
absolute zero 53
absorption spectra 56
accuracy 10
activation energy 31, 32
active transport 20
ADP 3
ALARA principle 2
alcohols 27, 29
alkanes 26
alleles 6, 16
alpha particle scattering 54
amino acids 17
animal fats 29
anomalous results 38
antagonistic pairs of muscles 8
antibiotics 22
antibodies 5
antigens 5
aperture 58
Apollo 59
aqueous solutions 34
arcseconds 50
atmosphere 21
atom economy 41
ATP 3, 4
atria 7
attractive strong force 55
autoradiography 24
autotrophs 13

B
bacteria 13, 22, 23
balancing equations 26
ball and stick representations 26
biceps 8
biomass 12-14, 43
biotechnology 22-24
black dwarfs 57
black holes 57
blood 4-7, 11
   donors 5
   flukes 15
   pressure 4
   transfusions 5, 16
   types 5, 6
body temperature 3
bond energies 32
bone marrow transplants 16
bones 8, 11
breathing 4
bulk chemicals 39

C
capillaries 7
carbon dioxide 3, 4, 7, 17-21, 26, 42
carboxylic acids 28, 29
carriers 16
cartilage 8
catalysts 30, 32, 42, 43
cells 3, 4, 7
   cell walls 17
cellulose 17
centre of curvature 49
Cepheid variable stars 50
chemical analysis 34
chemical synthesis 40
chlorophyll 17
chloroplasts 17
chromatography 35, 36
chromosomes 22, 24
   abnormalities 24
circulatory system 7
co-dominance 6
combustion 26
commensalism 15
compensation point 20
computer controlled telescopes 58
concave mirrors 58
   in telescopes 49
concentration 37
continuous spectra 56
controlled experiments 1
convection zone 55
converging lenses 48
convex lenses 48
core, of a star 55
covalent bonds 26

D
declination 47
decomposers 13
deforestation 21
diffraction in telescopes 58
diffusion 7
dioptres (D) 48
dislocations 11
distillation 30, 42
DNA 22-24
   complementary 24
Down syndrome 24
droughts 21
drugs 16
drying 30
dust 60
dynamic equilibrium 33, 35

E
Earth, orbit of 45
Earth, spin of 45
eclipses 46
eggs, human 6
emission spectra 56
endothermic reactions 31, 32
energy 3, 4, 13, 20, 31
   change 31
   costs 41
   energy level diagrams 31
   energy levels (in atoms) 56
enzymes 19, 22, 42
   restriction 23
esterification 29
esters 29, 30
ethanol 28, 42, 43
ethene 43
evidence 1
evolution 15
exercise 4, 11
exothermic reactions 31, 32
extended light sources 48
extract questions 62
eye lens 49

F
fair tests 1, 19
feedstocks, chemical 40
fermentation 42, 43
fermenters 22
filtration 30
fine chemicals 39
fitness 9-11
fluorescent DNA probes 24
focal length 48
focal point 48
food chains 12
fossil fuels 21
fractionating column 30, 42
full moon 46
functional groups 27-29
fungi 13, 22
fusion 55, 57

G
gas chromatography 36
gases, behaviour of 53
Geiger 54
gene probes 24
genes 6, 23
genetic diagrams 6
genetic disorders 24
genetic modification 22, 23

Index

genetic testing 24
genotype 6
global warming 21
glucose 3, 4, 7, 17, 20
gold foil experiment 54
graphs 64
gravitational collapse 57
greenhouses 19

H
health 9-11
health and safety 41
heart 7
   heart rate 4
heat exchangers 40
helium fusion 57
herbicides 23
heterotrophs 13
Hubble space telescope 59
human activity 21
hurricanes 21
hydrogen fusion 55, 57
hydroxides 27
hypotheses 1

I
inorganic material 14
insulin 23
intensity 56
International Space Station 60
intrinsic brightness 50
ionisation 33
ions 33
Isle of Wight 37

J
joints 8, 11

K
Kelvin scale of temperature 53

L
lactic acid 4
lenses 48
ligaments 8, 11
ligase 23
light 18-20
light pollution 60
limiting factors 18, 19
line of best fit 65
line spectra 56
liver 4
lunar eclipse 46
lungs 7

M
magnification 49
main sequence stars 57
malaria 15, 16
Marsden 54
medical history 9
microorganisms 23
minerals 14, 17, 20
mobile phase 35, 36
Moon 45, 46
mosquitoes 16
muscles 3, 4, 8, 11
mycoprotein 22

N
natural selection 16
neutralisation 28
neutron stars 57
new moon 46
nitrates 17
non-aqueous solutions 34
nuclear model of the atom 54
nucleus 22

O
objective lenses 49
   in telescopes 58
observatories 60
observed brightness 50
oxygen 3-5, 7, 14, 16, 17, 20, 22, 26
oxygen debt 4

P
pain 11
paper chromatography 35
paper three 65
parallax 50
parasitism 15, 16
parsecs 50
partial eclipse 46
patients 9
peak frequency 56
penicillin 22
perception 2
phases of the Moon 46
phenotype 6
photosphere 55
photosynthesis 13, 17-21
   rate of 18, 19
physiotherapists 11
planets 47
plants 12,-14, 17-20, 23
plasma 5

plasmids 22, 23
platelets 5
plum pudding 54
point light sources 48
power of a lens 48
precautionary principle 2
predictions 1
pressure 53
principal axis of a lens 48
producers 12
profitability 41
proteins 3, 17
protostars 57
pulse period 50
pulse rate 4
purification 30
purity 40
pyramids of biomass 12
pyramids of numbers 12

Q
qualitative analysis 34
quantitative analysis 34

R
rancid butter 28
recovery from illness/injury 10
red blood cells 5, 16
red giants 57
red supergiants 57
refluxing 30
refracting telescopes 49
rehabilitation from illness/injury 10
reliability 10, 19
remote telescopes 58
rennin 22
respiration 3, 4, 13, 14, 17, 20
   aerobic 3
   anaerobic 3, 4
reversible reactions 33
R_f values 36
RICE method 11
right ascension 47
risk 2
rocks 14
root hairs 20
Rutherford scattering 54

S
scientific process 1
sickle-cell anaemia 16
side effects 9, 10
sidereal day 45

Index and Answers

single covalent bonds 26
skeletal-muscular injuries 11
skeleton 8
sodium hydroxide 27
soil 14, 20
solar day 45
solar eclipse 46
solvents 27, 29
space telescopes 59
species 12
spectra 56
sprains 11
standard procedures 34
standard reference materials 36
standard solutions 37
starch 17
stars
   as seen from Earth 45
   structure of 55
stationary phase 35, 36
strong acids 28, 33
strong force 54
Sun 13, 45
supernovae 57
sustainability 41-43

sweaty socks 28
swelling 11
symbiosis 15
symptoms 9, 16
synovial fluid 8

T
telescopes 49, 58, 59
temperature 18, 19, 21, 22, 31
tendons 8, 11
theories 1
tissue fluid 7
titrations 38
treatments 10
triceps 8
trophic levels 12, 13

U
urea 7

V
variables 1, 19
vectors 23
vegetable oils 29
ventricles 7

vertebrates 8
vertex of a mirror 49
vinegar 28
viruses 23

W
waste biomass 43
waste products 41
water 3, 7, 14, 17, 18, 20
weak acids 28, 33
white blood cells 5, 24
white dwarfs 57
wine 28

Y
yeast 42

Z
zymase 42

Answers

Revision Summary for Module B7 (page 25)

23) Mass of soil before heating = 120 g − 25 g = 95 g
Mass of soil after heating = 105 g − 25 g = 80 g
Mass of water lost during heating = 95 g − 80 g = 15 g
Percentage of water in sample = (15 ÷ 95) × 100 = 15.8%

Revision Summary for Module C7 (page 44)

18) 4.5 ÷ 12 = <u>0.375</u>

22) 92 ÷ (650 ÷ 1000) = <u>141.5 g/dm^3</u>

24) b) Mass of KOH = 11.2 × (25 ÷ 1000) = 0.28 g
M_r of KOH = 39 + 16 + 1 = 56
M_r of HCl = 1 + 35.5 = 36.5
Mass of HCl ÷ M_r of HCl = Mass of KOH ÷ M_r of KOH
Mass of HCl ÷ 36.5 = 0.28 ÷ 56
Mass of HCl = 0.1825 g
Concentration of HCl = 0.1825 ÷ (48.9 ÷ 1000)
= <u>3.73 g/dm^3</u>

Revision Summary for Module P7 (page 61)

7) The focal point of a lens is where light rays initially parallel to the principal axis meet having passed through the lens.
Power = 1 ÷ focal length = 1 ÷ 0.4 = 2.5 D

11) Angular magnification = Power$_{eye}$ ÷ Power$_{objective}$
= 6.25 ÷ 0.4 = 15.625 = 15.6 (to 1 d.p.)

13) The parallax of a star is half the angle the star appears to move against distant background stars over six months.
distance = 1 ÷ parallax = 1 ÷ 0.5 = 2 pc

17) Speed of recession = Hubble constant × distance
= 2×10^{-18} × 2.4×10^{20} = 480 km/s

20) a) −89 °C = −89 + 273 = 184 K
b) 120 °C = 120 + 273 = 393 K
c) 5 °C = 5 + 273 = 278 K

Exam Skills (page 62)

1) a) If you repeat a measurement several times and get a similar result each time, it provides evidence that the data is reliable. The spread of values in a set of repeated measurements gives an indication of the range that the true value lies within.

b) No. The fourth value is much lower than the others (which are fairly similar).

c) (52 + 61 + 53 + 60) ÷ 4 = <u>56.5 micrograms per kg</u>

d) Yes. 56.5 micrograms per kg is well below the MRL of 10 000 micrograms per kg given in the article.

2) a) Phosmet will destroy pests and/or diseases which would otherwise damage crops.

b) Any one of: use natural predators such as ladybirds to control pests (biological control), use crop rotation to prevent the pests (and disease-causing organisms) of one particular crop plant building up in an area, leave field edges grassy to encourage larger insects and other animals that feed on pests, choose varieties of plants that are best able to resist pests and diseases, use natural pesticides responsibly.

3) Because pesticides may harm other organisms and residues on foods may harm humans.